Love PATCHWORK

SIMPLE PROJECTS & IDEAS FOR COLORFUL QUILTS, CUTE CUSHIONS, FRESH HOME STYLE, AND QUICK GIFTS

Love Patchwork is an original work, first published in 2012 in the United Kingdom by Future Publishing Limited in magazine form under the title *Love Patchwork*. This title is printed and distributed in North America under license. All rights reserved.

ISBN 978-1-57421-446-8

© 2013 by Design Originals, www.d-originals.com, an imprint of Fox Chapel Publishing, 800-457-9112, 1970 Broad Street, East Petersburg, PA 17520.

Printed in China
First printing

Love PATCHWORK

SIMPLE PROJECTS & IDEAS FOR COLORFUL QUILTS, CUTE CUSHIONS, FRESH HOME STYLE, AND QUICK GIFTS

EDITORS OF FUTURE PUBLISHING

Design Originals

an Imprint of Fox Chapel Publishing

www.d-originals.com

Love PATCHWORK

34

46

54

60

techniques
YOUR ESSENTIAL GUIDE TO
PATCHWORK
*Beginners will love our
handy, step-by-step guide
to all the essential sewing,
patchwork and quilting
techniques (see page 14)*

40

66 78

Exclusive!

*designer
profiles*

Introduction

WELCOME to the wonderful world of color, pattern and sheer gorgeousness that is patchwork! If you want to get the patchwork look, but don't know where to start, then you've come to the right place!

Once you start looking, there are lots of areas of your life that could benefit from a touch of **mix 'n' match** fabric. There's nothing nicer than watching the kids snuggling up under a **cozy handmade** throw on the sofa, or creating **instant heirlooms**, using recycled and scrap fabrics. You'll learn how **your own home** can be a source of **inspiration** and materials, while the **thrifty ideas** for **upcycling** worn clothes into brand-new accessories will have you creating **one-off gifts** in no time. Throughout the book are tips to make patchwork **fun and easy**, whether you're a stitching newbie, or already a sewing machine queen!

Browse the projects, features and inspiration that follow, and before you know it, you'll truly love patchwork!

Love PATCHWORK

CREATIVE INSPIRATION

Whether it's a pretty view, some favorite fabrics or a colorful bag of sweets – let your surroundings become the creative spark that inspires your next patchwork design

Craft designer Helen Philipps' pretty floral photograph features some gorgeous color combinations – for more inspiring images like this, visit Helen's blog at helenphilipps.blogspot.co.uk.

You don't have to look very far to find inspiration for patchwork. Have you ever noticed how a pile of washing can look really pretty with all the different colors jumbled together? And it's not just fabric – a stack of colored plates, a bunch of flowers, a bag of sweets – they can all feed your imagination and give you ideas for putting colors and patterns together. Take a look around – you're probably so completely surrounded by potential inspiration it's hard to choose what you like best! Read on for some great ways to pick out your inspiration from the world around you and translate it into fabulous patchwork...

The key to inspiration is knowing how to use it. You might love the way the beach looks, all dotted with people in summer clothes and deck chairs and beach balls, but how do you translate that into patchwork? Or you might feel inspired by a bag of jelly beans, but is it just the colors themselves or the way that lots of bright colors jumble together that get your creative juices flowing? Once you learn to delve under the surface of your inspiration you'll be off on a patchwork mission in no time!

PERFECT PATTERNS

So you've figured out what sort of colors you'd like to use in your quilt, but how do you work out how to get your favorite patterns in? Do you even know what your favorite patterns are? Chances are you've never asked yourself! Look again at your inspiration. Is it full of stripes? Does it contain a lot of curves? Is it a regimented arrangement of colors, or is it a jumble of shapes? Are there clear edges defining the shapes, or does one merge into the other, like

Use everyday images as your starting point – the colors and patterns in this photo show that green gingham might work well combined with a pink polka dot print and pink and yellow squares. Check out our 'Color Choices' flow chart to help you decide…

a watercolor painting? Once you've figured out the type of pattern that appeals to you most, you can choose fabrics that use those patterns AND your favorite colors to make patchwork that you will love!

MORE INSPIRATION

Still not feeling fired up? You need to get your 'art eyes' on. Find a quiet space, and make sure you've got five minutes to yourself (we know this can be easier said than done some days!). Take a deep breath, close your eyes, and imagine you're clearing your mind of all the visual clutter that's in there. Take another deep breath, and open your eyes. Keep them focused on the first thing you see, and look at it really carefully. Does the color change where there's a shadow? Is the shape simple or are there tiny details that you'd not noticed before? Keeping your 'art eyes' firmly in place, try leafing through magazines, searching the internet, or looking out of the window for images that you love. And once you settle on something that looks fabulous, you've found your inspiration. Congratulations!

COLOR CHOICES

Feel inspired by an image but not sure how to figure out why? Use this handy chart to figure out the color inspiration and you're halfway there!

START HERE! Think about the COLOR of your inspiration image

I like one particular color only

SORTED! Take that color and choose fabrics in different shades of it to create a harmonious quilt

I like two or more colors equally

The colors I like work well together without bringing anything else to the palette

They are too clashing

The colors I like don't look great together

SORTED! Find fabrics in your chosen contrasting palette to create your patchwork

SORTED! Separate colors with neutral tones such as beige or grey when arranging your patchwork

They are too cool

They are too warm

SORTED! Add a warm beige, yellow or cream into the mix when choosing fabric

SORTED! Add in a cool blue or grey to balance things up when choosing fabric

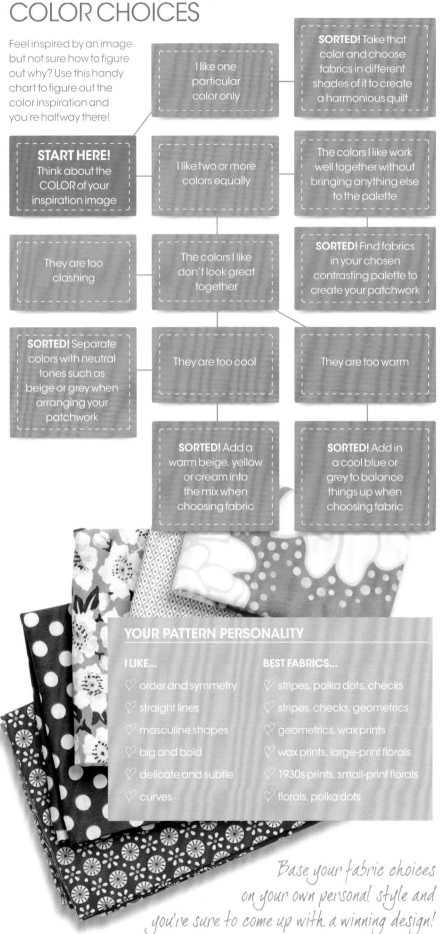

YOUR PATTERN PERSONALITY

I LIKE...	BEST FABRICS...
♡ order and symmetry	♡ stripes, polka dots, checks
♡ straight lines	♡ stripes, checks, geometrics
♡ masculine shapes	♡ geometrics, wax prints
♡ big and bold	♡ wax prints, large-print florals
♡ delicate and subtle	♡ 1930s prints, small-print florals
♡ curves	♡ florals, polka dots

Base your fabric choices on your own personal style and you're sure to come up with a winning design!

MAKING MEMORIES

Patchwork makes a great way to display precious fabrics with a history on a quilt or keepsake item, creating a family heirloom that will bring pleasure for years to come

Heirloom quilts have a timeless appeal and can be handed down from one generation to the next – this vintage fabric design comes from www. clothwork. blogspot.co.uk

Don't keep much-loved fabrics stored away and out of sight – use them for patchwork so they can be on display

how often have you kept hold of special clothes, blankets, curtains and cushions because they hold special memories? Maybe you couldn't quite bring yourself to send baby's first blanket or granny's apron off to the charity shop – but it seems such a shame to leave all this precious fabric packed in a box, or languishing at the back of a cupboard, never seeing the light of day. Well, get those boxes opened and those cupboards emptied, because it's time to make a meaningful heirloom quilt that you can not only display every day, but also hand down the generations!

It can feel very strange to cut into a treasured textile, but if something is simply no longer wearable or usable, then it's just good old recycling. Think of it as breathing new life into your fabric items, allowing them to evolve into something different that's both beautiful and useful. It's much better to reinvigorate and use something than to have it languishing at the

back of a closet, don't you think?

If you really can't bring yourself to cut something up, what about cleverly taking elements from it to use in a quilt? If you look carefully at a garment, for example, there could be pockets that you can gently undo – extra fabric on the inside of seams, spare buttons or even a beautiful vintage label.

Keep hold of buttons from a precious fabric item and give them a new lease of life, adding decoration to your patchwork.

ALL IN THE MIX

"Help! I don't have enough for a whole quilt" you shout. You've picked out all of the best details from your treasure trove of meaningful material, but it's only enough fabric in total to patch together a small napkin. Don't panic! We're here with the Dos and Don'ts for mixing your heirlooms with modern fabric.

♡ DO find modern fabric that is of a similar weight and fiber to your heirloom pieces

♡ DON'T pick background fabric with a pattern so vibrant it'll overwhelm your treasured keepsakes

♡ DO use a mix of different fabrics to make up the patchwork in similar colors and tones

♡ DON'T mix clashing colored fabrics or dark and light fabrics for the additional material

♡ DO use contrasting colored background fabrics if they'll set your treasures off nicely

♡ DON'T put all of your treasured pieces in one section of the patchwork; spread them out evenly for balance

DECORATIVE DETAILS

The most important thing to remember when selecting which parts of a treasured item to use in a patchwork quilt is detail, detail and detail! It's often the smallest things that mean the most to us: the smooth ribbon edge of a baby's blanket; the small butterflies in the print of great Aunt Edith's curtains; the breast pocket of granddad's shirt. And it's these very details that will remind you of the original item – and what it means to you.

Unpicking perfection

Use the right tools for the job: a stitch or seam ripper, or sharp embroidery scissors

EMBROIDERY AND MOTIFS

Embroidery – especially hand stitching – adds texture and color to your patchwork, and if you can re-use someone else's beautiful and painstakingly worked embroidery rather than put in the hours of labor yourself, then so much the better!

It's worth playing around with where to place these elements within a patchwork quilt, so that the overall look remains balanced. If in any doubt, simply put them in the middle.

BUTTONS AND BEADS

Buttons are a perfect detail to preserve from old items. Besides being a great element to save and recycle from a garment, vintage buttons often have a lot more character and quirkiness than shop bought ones, which adds further to their charm. If you can't easily keep a whole button band, remember you can detach buttons and then re-attach them in a new place. They make a great feature on any patchwork quilt, either at the intersection of four blocks or clustered in the corners. Play around and see what you like the look of best!

LABEL LOVE

It's always worth checking the labels on any vintage clothing or bedding – they can be really gorgeous! You don't have to make a whole patchwork quilt out of them either – you could simply include a few in your creation for added texture and interest.

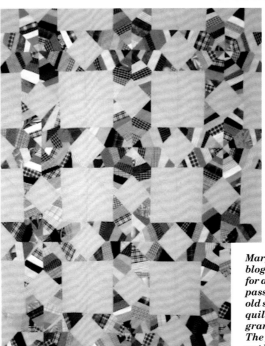

You don't have to give old clothes away – including them in a special patchwork quilt makes a wonderful way to remember a loved-one...

Mary Keasler (fiberliscious. blogspot.co.uk), made this quilt for a friend, who's husband had passed away, by cutting up his old shirts, "I also want to make a quilt for each child and each grandchild from his clothing. The youngest grandchild had not been born when he died, and I hope it will be a special keepsake for her as she grows up."

CREATIVE STYLE

Create a crafty corner in your home, where you can relax
and enjoy immersing yourself in your latest sewing project...

*Anri Lundqvist from Finland has created a
dedicated space for herself by arranging a blue
cupboard to partition off her craft area. You can
visit Anri's beautiful blog at anrinko.blogspot.co.uk*

WHEN STRAPPED FOR SPACE INDOORS *crafters have often set up their sewing spot in the garden! This pretty Gothic Shed is available from The Posh Shed Company.*

WELL- KNOWN ILLUSTRATOR
Jane Foster is also mad about fabric design and patchwork. Jane works from home in Devon and her craft space has a wonderful bold, retro feel – just like her designs! Find out more about Jane and her work, or shop for her goodies, by visiting www. janefoster.co.uk

H aving your own area to craft in is a luxury for some, but even a corner in the kitchen or a desk tucked in the spare room can act as a small haven, where you can indulge in your passion for patchwork in peace. If you've got the space, it really is worth having a room dedicated to crafting. Here you can store your fabrics and sewing equipment, display your designs and plan projects. Whether you buy new or second-hand, a good-sized table or desk, some deep shelves and storage boxes are a must. Check these craft rooms from sewing enthusiasts and see what ideas you can borrow.

AUSTRALIAN CRAFTER SHERIDAN
Powell, who blogs at chaletgirl. wordpress.com has a whole room to get creative in! We love the calming blue walls of Sheridan's craft room, the cute 'SEW' letters on the wall and, of course, Sheridan's patchwork sewing machine cover!

BRIGHT IDEAS
Set up station now…

1. The dining room table or kitchen bench are as good a sewing surface as anywhere – just wipe off any crumbs before laying out your fabric!

2. Check out second-hand stores and antique fairs for suitable work tables. Think about how you can utilize furniture – an old bureau would make a charming workstation for your machine, for example.

3. Storage, storage, storage. From shoeboxes and shelves to box files and biscuit tins, anything can help you to tidy away your sewing when family life reclaims the space!

4. Set up where there's good daylight – it makes such a difference to your sewing. Or try daylightcompany.com for crafty task lighting.

5. Make sure your cutting mat and ruler are the largest you can afford (and fit onto your workspace!).

SEW

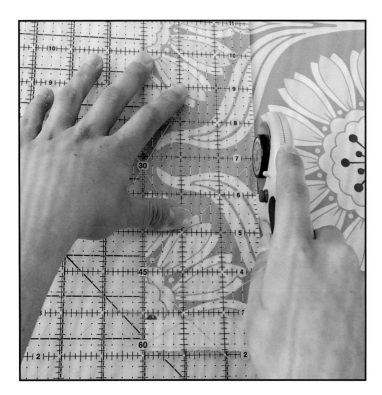

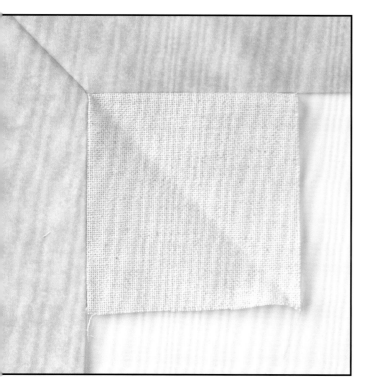
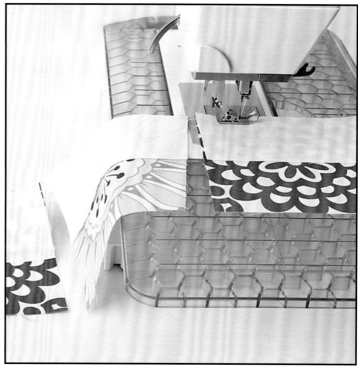

GETTING STARTED

Before beginning a patchwork project you'll want to reference this handy guide to the essentials on sewing, patchwork, and quilting techniques

essential sewing supplies

If you're totally new to sewing, there are a few essential items you'll need to stock up on – get yourself kitted out using our list below…

1 THREAD
There's a thread for almost every occasion and your local fabric store will help you find the right one for your project. Cotton is a great all-purpose thread, but polyester (or a mix) is worth using if you need extra strength.

2 BUTTONS
Buttons can be used for practical reasons, to secure the back of a cushion cover for instance, or just for decoration, such as to edge a blanket.

3 FASTENINGS
Safety pins can hold fabrics together when ordinary pins may fall out. Snap fasteners and other fastenings such as hooks and eyes may also be useful.

4 SEAM RIPPER
No matter how well you plan your stitches, there'll be some occasions when you need this handy gadget to help your undoing go smoothly and quickly.

5 THIMBLE
If you're regularly sewing or working with thicker fabrics, a thimble will save you from pricking your finger.

6 NEEDLEWORK SCISSORS
At about 13cm (5in) long, these are much smaller than fabric scissors. The fine, straight blade makes them good for trimming stray threads and removing excess fabric in tight spaces.

7 NEEDLES
You can get specialist needles for appliqué and quilting, but you'll also need a pack of assorted general-purpose sewing needles.

8 THREAD CUTTER
Use when travelling when you don't have the space for (or are not permitted to carry) scissors. If you plan to take a patchwork project on a flight, check the airline's restrictions before you travel.

9 FABRIC
If you're after a specific amount of fabric, you'll find it is sold by the yard or meter. However, if you're looking for a variety of fabric patterns to patchwork, you can also buy a 'fat quarter'. This is a piece of fabric measuring about 18 x 22in (a yard cut into four sections), which can be bought individually or in bundles.

10 PINS
Use these to hold your pieces of fabric together. Regular dressmakers' pins can be fiddly, so it's worth getting pins with larger glass or 'flower' heads – these lie flat so you can iron over them. Use special quilting pins for quilting.

11 FABRIC SCISSORS
Keep your scissors sharp by only using them for fabric. Look for some that are about 20cm (8in) long and have a curved handle to enable accurate cutting on flat surfaces, with pointed tips for precision.

12 TAPE MEASURE
Measuring fabric correctly is one of the essential elements of creating a perfect patchwork design (measure twice, cut once!), so make sure you buy one that measures around 150cm (60in) and has both metric and imperial units for quick conversions. Some have different colored sections to make measuring even easier.

USEFUL PATCHWORK TOOLS

Besides your general sewing kit, there are some other tools you'll also need to help your patchwork making go smoothly as possible…

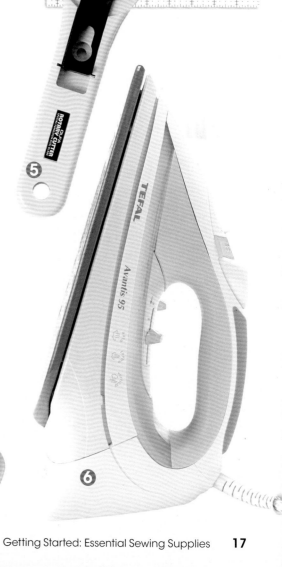

1 CUTTING MAT & RULER

A cutting mat protects your work surface while you're using a rotary cutter. Most are 'self-healing' (meaning that any scratches disappear after use) and are printed with gridlines to help you align your fabrics. You'll also need an acrylic patchwork ruler, which come in a variety of shapes and widths.

2 PINKING SHEARS

Some woven fabrics can fray easily, but you can help prevent this by cutting them with a pair of pinking shears. These leave a zig-zag edge that is great for storing fabrics and also makes a great decorative effect. Choose a pair that has steel blades and a contoured handle, so that they're comfortable to work with.

3 TAILOR'S CHALK

Before you start stitching, you may need something to transfer guidelines onto your fabric. Tailor's chalk is ideal for this because it goes on and comes off easily – so easily, in fact, that you may need to be careful you don't brush it off by accident. Choose basic white or a colored chalk if you're working with pale fabrics.

4 FABRIC PENCIL

While tailor's chalk is a great marking material, you may find you have more choice with fabric pencils. These come in many different shades, so you can find the color that stands out best on your material. Chalk pencils often have a brush for erasing unwanted lines, while water-soluble pencils come out in the wash.

5 ROTARY CUTTER

Used to cut fabric, these are extremely sharp and should be kept away from children. They're popular with quilters because they can cut several layers of material at once and give more even results than scissors. Decide what size blade you need before you buy – small diameters tend to be better at cutting curves.

6 IRON

Crumpled fabrics can cause stitching mishaps, so you'll usually need to press your material before you sew. An iron is also useful for flattening seams and, of course, getting rid of unwanted creases. Use an ironing cloth or a tea towel to protect delicate fabrics when you iron them, and iron them on the reverse side.

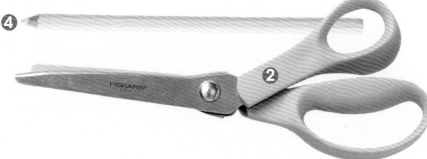

patchwork techniques

Before you begin your first project, read patchwork expert Elizabeth Hartman's guide to cutting and piecing…

Pages 18–22 (from Rotary Cutting Basics to Pressing Seams): All text, images and associated content are taken from *The Practical Guide to Patchwork* by Elizabeth Hartman. See page 22 for details.

PREPARING FABRIC

Whether you are using up old pieces of fabric, or working with new pieces, make sure you hand-wash your scraps in pure soap. This is essential, as not only will you have clean fabric to work with, but any fabric shrinkage will take place at this stage, before the joining of your pieces, and thus avoiding any puckering.

Vintage fabrics will also benefit from being starched, ensuring that your project will have a crisp finish, as old fabrics often soften with age and wear. Always press your fabric before you cut it.

NOTE

These instructions are written for right-handed people, and the photos show a right-handed person cutting. If you're left-handed, you'll want to do the opposite of what is described here, including moving the rotary cutter blade to the opposite side of the cutter.

ROTARY CUTTING BASICS

Rotary cutters are essential for ensuring your fabric pieces are cut as accurately as possible. Follow our step-by-step guides in order to use them correctly and safely

SAFETY FIRST!

Before we start with cutting, let's talk about safety. Rotary cutter blades are very sharp and can cut you as easily as they cut fabric. Most cutters have a button to lock the position of the blade, and it's a good idea to get in the habit of using it. As you cut, keep all your fingers on the hand that's not holding the cutter on top of the ruler and out of the path of the cutter.

LINE IT UP *Always line up your ruler with the grain of the fabric and keep your hand on top of the ruler and out of the path of the cutter.*

Rotary cutting should, in general, be done from a standing position. The vantage point gained by standing and the additional pressure you'll be able to put on the ruler will make for more accurate cutting. If possible, use your rotary cutter on a table that you can walk all the way around. This will minimize the number of times you have to move the fabric you're cutting. All fabric should be free from wrinkles prior to cutting. This is essential for accurate cutting, so take the time to press your fabric before you work with it.

Unless otherwise noted in the directions, the ruler should always be lined up with the grain of the fabric. Hold it firmly in

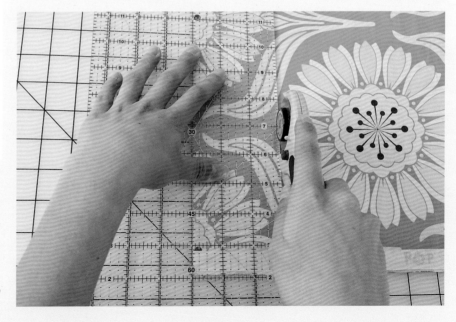

place with your left hand, keeping all your fingers on top of the ruler and out of the path of the cutter.

Prepare to cut by lining up the blade with the right edge of the ruler. Use even pressure to run the cutter along the edge of the ruler, making a clean cut through the fabric. As you cut, keep your fingers clear of the blade.

The first cuts you make from your fabric will usually be strips cut along the width or the length of the fabric. In most cases these strips are then cut into smaller pieces.

Cutting along the width (selvedge to selvedge) is easier and is how most pieces are cut. Cutting along the length (cut edge to cut edge) of the fabric is used to make longer sashing or border strips or backing pieces.

CUTTING ALONG THE WIDTH OF THE FABRIC

1 Fold the fabric selvedge to selvedge and place it on the cutting mat with the folded edge nearest you.

2 Lay a 6 × 24in ruler on top of the fabric. Match a horizontal line on the ruler to the fold and slide the ruler near the cut edge on the right side of the fabric.

3 Cut off a small strip of fabric along the right side of the ruler, creating a straight edge at a right angle to the fold. This is called 'squaring up' the fabric.

4 Move to the opposite side of the table (or, if you cannot, carefully turn your rotary cutting mat around). Now the straight edge you just cut is on the left side of the fabric, and the folded edge away from you.

5 Use the lines on the ruler to measure the width of the strip you want to cut and, again, cut along the right side of the ruler. Continue making cuts, moving from left to right across the fabric.

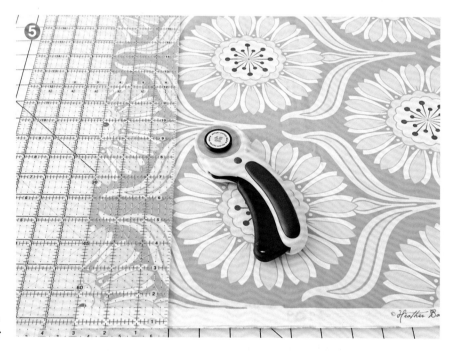

Change your rotary cutter blade regularly. Dull or nicked blades make accurate cutting more difficult and can cause ugly little pulls in the fabric

CUTTING ALONG THE LENGTH OF THE FABRIC

Since fabric is usually about 42–44in wide, strips longer than this need to be cut along the length of the fabric (parallel to the selvedge edge). To make an accurate cut, you'll first need to refold the fabric to a size that will fit on your mat.

Instead of folding the fabric along the existing fold, fold it in the opposite direction, bringing the cut edges together and matching the selvedges along one side. Fold the fabric once or twice more, continuing to keep the selvedges along one side lined up, until you can easily lay the fabric on your cutting mat.

You may need to let one end of the fabric hang off the end of the table. Just be careful not to let its weight pull the nicely folded edge out of alignment. You may need to set a book or something else heavy on the folded fabric, out of the way of your cutting tools.

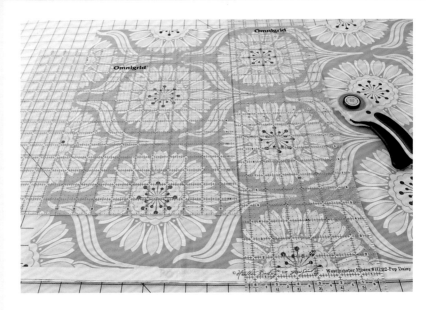

WHAT IF MY RULER ISN'T WIDE ENOUGH?

Some of the patterns require larger pieces than you'll be able to cut with a 6 × 24in ruler alone. In those cases, use a 12 ½in square ruler to add extra width. When you do this, always keep the 6 × 24in ruler on the right edge of the square ruler and cut along the narrow ruler's 24in edge.

Trim away the selvedge to square the edge and use this as the straight edge to cut the pattern pieces. You'll be cutting through more layers than you would if you were cutting along the width, so be careful and realign the edge of the fabric as necessary.

FUSSY CUTTING

Fussy cutting is the common term for cutting a print fabric in such a way as to center or otherwise highlight a particular part of the print.

Cut a piece of translucent template plastic (available at most quilt or craft shops) in the size of the piece you need and move it around the surface of the fabric until you find the part you want to highlight (see left). Keep in mind that when you stitch the piece, you'll lose ¼in on each side to the seam allowance.

Trace around the outside of the template with a disappearing-ink marker and use the marked lines to cut out the piece with either scissors or a ruler and rotary cutter.

Because you're using only certain parts of the print, fussy cutting takes up quite a bit more fabric than standard rotary cutting, so you'll need to buy roughly twice as much of any fabric that you plan to fussy cut.

MEASUREMENTS NOTE

In Love PATCHWORK *you'll find that either imperial or metric measurements are included in a project – or sometimes both. Converting all projects to metric could actually interfere with the accuracy of the fabric cutting. Pinpoint cutting accuracy is crucial for many patchwork designs to work, so we recommend you always use the measurements system stated within the project you are working on.*

PATCHWORK PIECING BASICS

Taking the time to ensure your patchwork pieces are joined together with an accurate seam allowance can be the crucial difference between a project's failure and success…

The patterns some of the designers have created in this magazine reflect a preference for hard edges and sharp, precise piecing. In order to achieve this look, it's important to remember that every step of the process matters. The accuracy of your seam allowances, the way you press the seams, and whether or not you square up your blocks are all-important to duplicating this look.

However, there is absolutely no reason you can't take a more relaxed approach. If you prefer a wonky look or just aren't too concerned about having seams match up exactly, go for it! If you do go down this route, keep in mind that your blocks will probably end up being different sizes than the pattern states, so it's best to wait until after you finish the blocks to cut out any sashing pieces.

SEAM ALLOWANCE

Learning to sew an accurate seam allowance is one of the keys to successful patchwork piecing. Most quilt patterns, call for a ¼in seam allowance – but it's not always the case – we recommend you always check the actual project instructions each time to see what seam allowance it asks for.

Many quilters use the edge of the presser foot as a guide, but beware that foot sizes vary, and yours may not be exactly ¼in wide.

STITCH QUALITY

Sew the patchwork pieces together using a small to medium stitch length. We prefer the 2 to 3 setting on our sewing machine, which appears to be about 12 stitches per inch. Before you start sewing on your quilt fabric, test your machine's stitch on scrap fabric and make adjustments if necessary.

In general, if the top of your project looks puckered and the bobbin thread appears

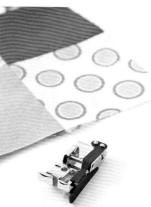

SIMPLE SEAMS
Patchwork quilts such as this need an accurate seam allowance – you can use a ¼in foot on your machine (below) to help you achieve this.

to be pulled in a straight line, the thread tension is too tight. If the top thread and bobbin thread are loopy, the thread tension may be too loose. We recommend consulting your machine's manual when making any tension adjustments.

BEFORE YOU ADJUST THE TENSION …

If your stitch is bad, the first thing to do is change your needle. Always – even if you haven't been using that needle for very long. (Sometimes even a brand-new needle can create poor-quality stitches.)

Needles do a lot of work, and even the smallest nick can affect their performance.

Another thing to check is the thread. We cannot stress enough the importance of using quality thread. Switching to a better thread can make a huge difference in stitch quality.

Last but not least, check the bobbin. Take out the bobbin casing and make sure there are no loose threads caught around it. Make sure the bobbin is wound properly and then place it back in the machine.

PINNING

It's best to pin all your patchwork pieces before sewing, inserting pins through all the layers on both sides of each seam allowance. Keep a pincushion next to your machine and remove pins as you sew. All this pinning may seem tedious, but it will lead to accuracy.

When sewing together a solid piece of fabric (for instance, a piece of sashing) and a pieced block, always keep the pieced block on top. This will help you keep an eye on the block's seam allowances and ensure that they don't get pulled askew by your machine's feed dogs

Left: Always pin your work before you start sewing. Center: Save time using the chain piecing technique. Right: Iron your seams flat for a smoother finish.

CHAIN PIECING

A great way to save both time and thread, chain piecing is sort of like running a mini assembly line. Gather similar pairs of pieces and run them through your machine one after the other, without stopping to clip the threads between pieces. When you're done, clip the threads between each set and press as usual.

PRESSING SEAMS

Press your seams open. It takes a bit more effort than pressing to the side, as many quilters do, but the results are worth it. Your finished blocks will be more precise, will lie flatter, and will be easier to machine quilt in an all-over pattern. The even distribution of the seam allowances should also ensure that the quilt wears more evenly.

Lay your work right side down on the pressing surface and use your index finger to press open the seam. Follow this by running the point of your iron down the seam. Then place the entire iron over

the seam and press firmly, adding a little burst of steam. Flip the work over and gently iron the front (right) side.

For long seams you can lay your work face-up on the pressing surface, press to one side, and then flip the project over to press the seam open.

Some quilters believe that pressing seams open will have a negative impact on the structural integrity of the quilt.

But, as long as you're using a good stitch and good materials, a quilt made with pressed-open seams should be perfectly sturdy.

Pressing to the side is easier, and many quilters like it for this reason. If you're a devoted side presser, we may not be able to change your mind. But it's worth giving open pressing a try, as many quilts will be most successful with open pressing.

Pages 18–22 (from Rotary Cutting Basics to Pressing Seams): All text, images and associated content are taken from ***The Practical Guide to Patchwork* by Elizabeth Hartman, published by Stash Books.** Twelve contemporary quilt designs for beginners, confident beginners and intermediates. Learn how to cut, piece, appliqué, machine quilt, bind and finish.

QUILTING

Patchwork and quilting often go hand in hand, but are really two separate techniques. If you are intending to turn your patchwork into a quilt, check out our advice on how to finish your work…

HOW TO SEW MITRED CORNERS

You'll need four strips of fabric – one for each edge. Pin one border strip to one side of the main piece of fabric, right sides together, making sure it's centrally placed. Sew together, using a 1.5cm (½in) seam allowance. Attach the other three strips to each side in the same way. Take care not to stitch into the fabric strips that are already attached.

1 Working one corner at a time, fold one strip over the other and pin. Using a pencil, draw a line on the fabric at 45 degrees from the inner corner.

2 Swap over the positions of the border strips and repeat the process.

3 With right sides together, match up the pencil lines and pin. Stitch the borders together along this line. Trim off the excess border strips and press the seam open.

4 Mitre the other corners in the same way. To finish, place the main fabric and backing fabrics together, right sides facing, and sew together with a 1.5cm (½in) seam allowance. Leave a gap at the bottom so you can turn it out the right way. Trim the corners and edges, then turn the right way out. Slip stitch the gap closed.

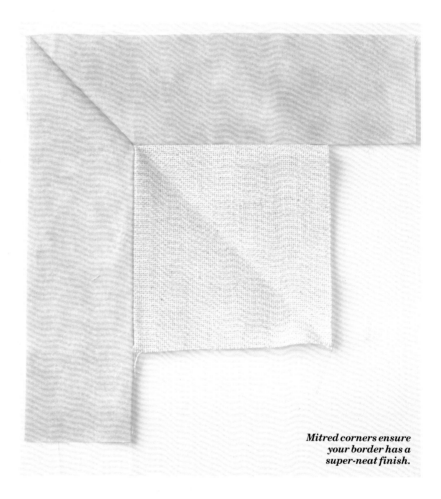

Mitred corners ensure your border has a super-neat finish.

MAKING A QUILT SANDWICH

To make a quilt you are simply layering and joining a backing, central batting (or wadding) and quilt top (such as your patchwork) together.

1 Press your backing and lay on a flat surface, wrong side up. Use masking tape to hold it taut, without stretching it.

2 Add your batting over the backing, centring it and smoothing out any wrinkles.

3 Repeat with the quilt top, which should be right side up, ensuring the top quilt layer's top edge is lined up with the top edge of the backing.

4 Pin your quilt together, starting from the center – insert a pin around every 4in.

You are now ready to start quilting – and it's really up to you how you go about this. You could follow the seams of your patchwork pieces (this is called 'stitching in the ditch') – or you could quilt in rows for a more contemporary look – you'll need a walking foot on your sewing machine for either of these options.

Or you can simply 'quilt as desired' – which involves working freehand stitching in patterns of your choice over your quilt, adding an extra decorative effect at the same time. If you're going to give freehand quilting a go, you'll need to use a darning foot on your machine (see page 26).

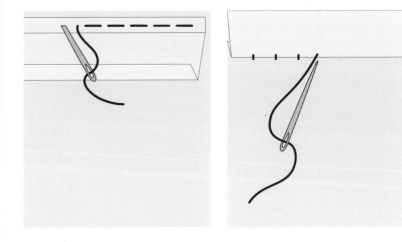

HOW TO SEW ON BIAS BINDING

Bias binding is a strip of fabric cut on the bias (diagonally) so that it stretches and follows curves well. Use it to give edges a neat finish.

1 Unfold the tape and position the slightly wider side of it along the edge of the right side of the fabric. Use your machine to stitch it into place, or hand sew, along the entire length of the fabric edge.

2 Fold over the edge onto the reverse, then slip stitch in place by hand. Use tiny stitches and don't go through the top layer of bias binding.

Once your patchwork quilt top is complete, you can move on to the actual quilting process. This involves making a quilt sandwich, quilting your layers together, and then providing a firm edging for your quilt by either sewing on bias binding (above) or attaching a fabric border with mitred corners for a neat finish (left)

more useful techniques

Now you've got the patchwork and quilting basics covered, here are a few extra sewing skills that will also come in handy…

FUSIBLE INTERFACING

Flimsy fabric can be stiffened and given extra strength by backing it with interfacing. You can buy regular interfacing that you sew into your project, or you can get the fusible kind, which means that you iron it on. The fusible interfacing will have a shiny, bumpy side and a smooth side. The bumpy side has adhesive on it – and this side needs to be placed on the wrong side of your fabric, then ironed on. Take care not to let it pucker the fabric, because you won't be able to remove it afterward.

USING TEMPLATES

Several projects in *Love PATCHWORK* use templates. Check the project instructions for details of how much you may need to enlarge your template on a photocopier. Sometimes templates need to be flipped, such as if you are creating a front and back for an item.

You can transfer your template outline onto your fabric by using a window as a lightbox. Tape your paper template to a window using masking tape, then attach tracing paper to the wrong side of the fabric the design will be applied to. Now tape the tracing paper-backed fabric over the design on the window and use a water-soluble pen or pencil to trace the design on top of your fabric. Alternatively, cut them out and pin to your fabric, as described in individual project instructions.

APPLYING APPLIQUÉ MOTIFS

For larger appliqué motifs, it's best to pin them in place on the background fabric before sewing them on. You could use fabric glue instead of pins for very small pieces – just take care not too use too much, or things will get messy. Or you could tack motifs in place with a contrasting thread, which you can remove later on.

Another option is to use fusible webbing. Fusible webbing is a paper-backed heat-sensitive film that you iron onto the wrong side of the fabric. You then draw and cut out the shape of the motif, remove the paper backing and iron your motif in place onto your background fabric. You will then need to also sew around your appliqué motif to secure it.

A cute cushion featuring pretty appliqué hearts.

Use fusible webbing to attach your motif.

BLANKET STITCH

Give appliqué motifs a decorative finish by sewing them onto your base material using this pretty embroidery stitch. Pull the needle through to form a loop. The vertical stitches should be evenly spaced and of the same length. It may help to draw parallel lines onto the fabric.

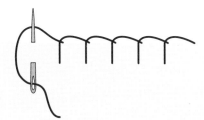

Adding blanket stitch edging or freehand machine stitched embroidery to your appliqué motifs will help give them an individual, homespun look

FREEHAND MACHINE STITCHING

Sometimes you'll need to use your sewing machine to make freehand stitching – this simply means that you're no longer working straight lines, and have more freedom to 'doodle' with your machine and work the stitch in any direction. This is great for when you want to add an arty touch to appliqué motifs – you'll need a darning (or free-motion) foot for your sewing machine. The darning foot will also allow you to quilt in random patterns, if you desire. Before you start stitching you'll also need to drop the feed dogs on your machine, to allow your fabric to move freely as you stitch.

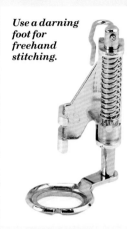

Use a darning foot for freehand stitching.

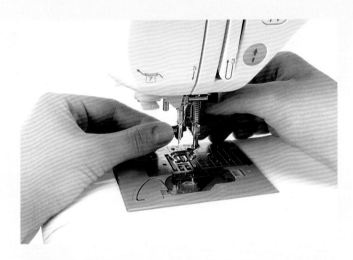

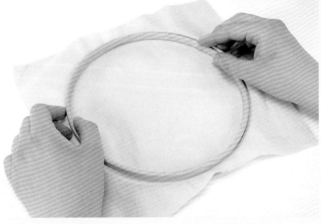

Purchase a darning foot, which can often be picked up at your local sewing shop. Consult your sewing machine manual for specific instructions on attaching your darning foot, because all machines are different.

Mount your fabric onto a wooden stitch hoop, the opposite way to normal, so the inner ring is facing up. Lift up your darning foot and place your hoop underneath. Drop the feed dogs, thread your needle, and you're ready.

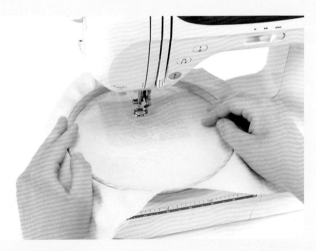

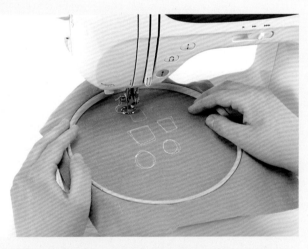

Hold the hoop firmly with both hands. Begin sewing, moving the hoop in any direction. Use scrap fabric to practice making squiggles and shapes. It takes a while to get the hang of it, so don't get discouraged.

Once you feel a bit more confident, try stitching some shapes, starting with squares. Then move on to circles, and finally hearts. We've worked all our designs using double outlines, which creates a wonderful, sketchy look.

MY LIFE WITH PATCHWORK!

Designer extraordinaire Amy Butler reveals the ten ways that patchwork plays a part in her life, and shares ideas to help us live the patchwork life too!

1 PILLOW TALK

Pillows and cushions play a big role in my home décor and I love mixing patchwork designs in with my prints and solid colors to create a warm and interesting combination on my couches.

2 MADE WITH LOVE

Quilts are a huge love of mine and I enjoy bringing them into our home and also gifting them to friends and family. I love the soulful energy in patchwork quilts and the history and heritage that backs the spirit of this gorgeous art form. Made by hand with heart is the ultimate gift we can give ourselves and others.

3 BRIGHT IDEA!

Dave and I love to take little road trips or day adventures and I always have a quilt in the car to lay out on the ground when we find the perfect picnic spot under a shady tree.

Photos: Images © David Butler

4 **TIME FOR TEA**
Entertaining at home is one of my great pleasures. Using patchwork to create little accessories like napkins and table cloths to match party decor is another great way to bring a special feeling to your gathering.

5 **BRIGHT IDEA!**
I love to cook and the kitchen is the heart of our house, where patchwork is particularly at home with aprons made up in colorful combinations and loads of hot pads on hand... I love hot pads [mini quilts]. Patchwork has such a connecting energy all about it and it brings in the perfect touches of warmth that make everyone feel cared for and special.

IN BLOOM, ONLINE!

I am so excited to announce the release of my new free, online magazine this month! *Blossom* is a visual journal that's all about loving your life and living it beautifully. Filled with loads of creative ideas and inspirations, Blossom celebrates our creative expression and passions, our mantra is: '*Create Love, Be Kind and Express Beauty*'. I can't wait for you to connect with the joy!
– Amy XO
www.amybutlerdesign.com/ blossommagazine

6 **SITTING PRETTY**
Patchwork looks beautiful when it's used to upholster furniture including chairs and sofas. I've made several patchwork chair and seat covers in the past to highlight my fabric collections. The best bit is the chair quickly finds a home in my living room after the show!

»

7 SEW STYLISH

Patchwork and fashion are perfect together! I love using patchwork techniques when I am making clothes. It allows you to combine so many various colors and patterns to make a truly unique garment.

8 ON THE ROAD

I travel a lot so I am always in need of pouches to keep all of my small items together. Fun colors and pattern combinations make me smile every time I open up my suitcase.

9 BRIGHT IDEA!

I love giving gifts to friends and family at any time of the year. Using up fabric scraps in fun patchwork designs to use for wrapping my packages is so much fun. It's like giving an extra gift before they even open the box!

10 ARM CANDY

Another great place to express yourself with patchwork is through your personal accessories, such as with scarves, bags, and even jewellery. What's fun about working on patch projects of this scale is that you can also play with adding luscious details like adding embroidery or beading.

FIND OUT MORE!

Visit Amy at www.amybutlerdesign.com for more information about her fabric collections, patterns and other products. You'll also discover free patterns, inspiration and lots more eye candy.

Photos: Images © David Butler

PROJECTS

Make a creative style statement by introducing the vibrant colors and patterns or patchwork into your home and gift giving crafts.

very berry rug

designed by Emma Hardy

YOU WILL NEED

- ☐ Selection of fabrics each at least 100cm (40in) long

- ☐ White cotton fabric at least 100cm (40in) long by the width of the finished rug

- ☐ Heavyweight cotton wadding at least 100cm (40in) long by the width of the finished rug

- ☐ Backing fabric at least 120cm (48in) long and 20cm (8in) wider than the finished rug

- ☐ Basic sewing kit (see page 16)

- ☐ Seam allowance: 1cm (½in)

Lay this rug by the fireplace, next to the bed, or on a chilly bathroom floor to stay warm and cozy underfoot!

Strips of fabric in different widths, colors and patterns have been used to make this striking rug. Lined with medium-weight wadding and backed with a heavyweight cotton, it will stand up to family wear and tear.

This is a great way to mix different scales of patterns. Big retro florals and graphic circles next to small-scale posies and gingham work together because of the purple palette. Dashes of contrasting teal and green are punchy but minimal – perfect!

Great for first-time pattern mixers!

1 Measure and cut strips of fabric in varying widths all 100cm (40in) long and at least 10cm (4in) wide. Lay them onto the work surface in a pleasing arrangement. With right sides together, pin and stitch the strips together, pressing the seams open as you work. Add more strips if you would like a wider rug.

2 Cut the wadding and white cotton fabric to the same size as the patchwork panel. Lay the cotton onto the work surface with the wadding on the top and the patchwork on top of that right side up. Pin all the layers together to hold them in place. Machine stitch along the seams to quilt the layers together.

A SPLASH OF *teal is a wonderful accent against lilac and plum!*

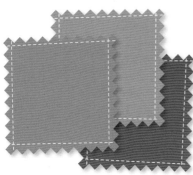

TOP TIP
Pressing the seams as you work will make adding each strip faster and more accurate.

Imagine how beautiful this little rug would look next to your sofa or favorite armchair – your floor will love you for it!

Text © Emma Hardy; Photographs © Loupe Images/Debbie Patterson; Artwork © Loupe Images/Michael Hill

Use darker colored fabrics if your rug will get lots of wear and tear!

3 For the backing, cut a piece of fabric measuring 120cm (48in) long and 10cm (4in) wider on each side than the patchwork panel. Press under 1cm (½in) all the way round it. Lay it on the work surface wrong side up and place the quilted patchwork panel centrally onto it, right side up. Turn over the backing fabric overlapping the raw edge of the patchwork by 1cm (½in) and pin in place to create the border. Machine stitch in place and repeat along the opposite side.

4 Repeat step 3 along the two remaining ends of the rug, pinning the border in place and machine stitching to finish. Press.

Pages 32–33: This project and all associated text, images and patterns taken from *Quilting in No Time* by Emma Hardy, published by CICO Books. Visit www.cicobooks.com

pretty-in-pink cushions

designed by Corinne Crasbercu

DREAMS CUSHION

YOU WILL NEED

☐ Ten pieces of cotton fabric in different prints, for the front of the cushion

☐ 56 x 4cm (22 x 1½in) strip of white lace

☐ 62 x 2cm (24½ x ¾in) strip of white lace

☐ Two strips of one of the printed fabrics for the front, each 50 x 6cm (19¾ x 2¼in), for the bows

☐ Two rectangles pink cotton, 59 x 42cm (23 x 16½in) and 23 x 42cm (9 x 16½in), for the back

☐ Basic sewing kit (see page 16)

☐ Seam allowance: 1cm (½in)

CUT OUT

Following the sizes indicated on the placement diagram on page 38, cut out the rectangles and squares from the printed fabrics, adding a 1cm (½in) margin all around each piece to allow for the seams

Filling your home with patchwork is most easily done with cushions – on chairs, on beds, on the floor…

The possibilities for using cushions and pillows are endless! Simple cushions are also a great way to try out patchwork ideas, use up fabric odds and ends, and experiment with embellishment techniques.

These cushions include some simple hand embroidery, appliqué and machine zig-zag stitch. The Dreams cushion is made up of various scraps of fabric, trims and a touch of hand embroidery. If you fancy trying out some simple appliqué, then the Flowers cushion is for you. Take your time cutting out the pieces and attaching them, and the result is stunning.

Once you feel more confident, you can have a go at mixing up the techniques to create some custom-made cushions – there's nothing like a unique, one-off accessory to make your home feel special.

Designer trick – mix + match ideas!

CANDY STORE PINK *punctuated with reds and greens is a fresh take on pretty!*

Spots, checks, strips and florals are the classic fabric combo for the rustic homespun look. Embellishing the patchwork with cotton lace makes it extra special.

dreams

If you have a particularly beautiful fabric piece you'd like to use, put it in the center of your patchwork and place the rest of the fabric pieces around it

Pages 34–39: This project and all associated text, images and patterns taken from *Made in France: Everything Patchwork* by Corinne Crasbercu, published by Murdoch Books. Visit www.murdochbooks.co.uk

1 With right sides together and allowing 1cm (½in) seams, sew the cut-out pieces to each other as shown in the diagram. Make up the front in two blocks: the large square-ish shape on the left and the vertical strip to the right. Then sew the two sections together for the finished front of the cushion. When you are sewing the fabric together, remember to sew the edges of the lace into the seams at the same time.

2 Embroider the word 'dreams' using stem stitch (see below) in the top right-hand rectangle. Separate out two strands of embroidery thread to do this. Embroider some stars, as shown, with straight stitches. This time, make sure you use all strands of your length of embroidery thread.

TOP TIP

Don't worry about attaching the lace and ribbon too perfectly. Both can be tricky to work with as the straight lines are very unforgiving. However, if you aim for a homespun look and allow yourself the freedom for a few wobbly lines, you'll enjoy the process so much more!

3 Press under 1cm (½in) and then another 1cm (½in) on one 42cm (16½in) edge of each back section and stitch the hem in place. Lay the two hemmed pieces out, right side up, with the hemmed edges overlapping, to make a piece measuring 62 x 42cm (24½ x 16½in). Place the front piece of the cushion on top of the back, right sides together. Stitch all around, 1cm (½in) from the edge, turn right side out and press.

4 Make two ties using strips of printed fabric (about 6cm [2½in] wide and 50cm [19¾in] long). Fold the strip of fabric in half lengthways, right sides together, and stitch along the length and one of the short ends, 1cm (½in) from the edge. Turn right side out using a knitting needle to push out the corners. Turn in the fabric on the open end and sew close with invisible stitches. If the ties are too narrow to be turned out, press under 5mm (⅛in) on each side and end, fold the fabric in half lengthways, wrong sides together, and stitch along the edges, 1mm (¹⁄₁₆in) from the edge.

5 Sew the ties to the right-hand edge of the cushion at evenly spaced intervals and tie them into bows. And you're done! Sit back, relax and admire your creation.

HOW TO... STEM STITCH

This stitch is worked horizontally, from left to right. Bring the needle out on the right side of the fabric, then reinsert to the right and bring out again in the middle of these two points. Keep going in the same way all along the outline to be embroidered, making one neat continuous line, and always keeping the thread underneath the row of stitches (to the right of the needle).

If you're not confident about your stitching abilities, or simply prefer not to add embroidery, you could embellish this patch with buttons or more lace if desired

Pom-pom trim is so versatile – use single balls as shown here, or attach whole lengths to trim cushions and blankets.

FLOWERS CUSHION

YOU WILL NEED

☐ Double-sided fusible appliqué webbing, for the print fabrics

☐ Seven pieces of cotton fabric in different prints, for the letters

☐ 62 x 37cm (24½ x 14½in) pale pink cotton, for the front

☐ Two rectangles of pale pink cotton, 24 x 37cm (9½ x 14½in) and 60 x 37cm (23½ x 14½in), for the back

☐ Four small dark pink pom-poms

☐ Basic sewing kit (see page 16)

☐ Seam allowance: 1cm (½in)

1 Trace the letters of the word 'FLOWERS' (see page 39) back-to-front onto the paper side of the double-sided appliqué webbing and cut out roughly. Fuse the webbing to the wrong side of the printed fabrics, then cut out accurately (see appliqué instructions on page 25). Remove the backing paper from each letter and fuse the letters to the large rectangle of pink cotton.

2 Machine-sew around the outline of the letters in zigzag stitch. Next, embroider the outline of the F, W, R and S in blanket stitch (see techniques on page 25) using two strands of dark pink stranded cotton.

3 Press under 1cm (½in) and then another 1cm (½in) on one 37cm (14½in) edge of each section of the back and stitch the hem in place. Lay the two hemmed pieces out, right side up and with the hemmed edges overlapping, to make a rectangle measuring 62 x 37cm (24½ x 14½in).

4 Place the front piece of the cushion on top of the back, right sides together. Stitch all around, 1cm (½in) from the edge, turn right side out and press. To finish, sew a small pink pom-pom to each corner of the cushion.

Turn over for your cutting guide and template

DREAMS CUSHION cutting guide

All measurements are in cm

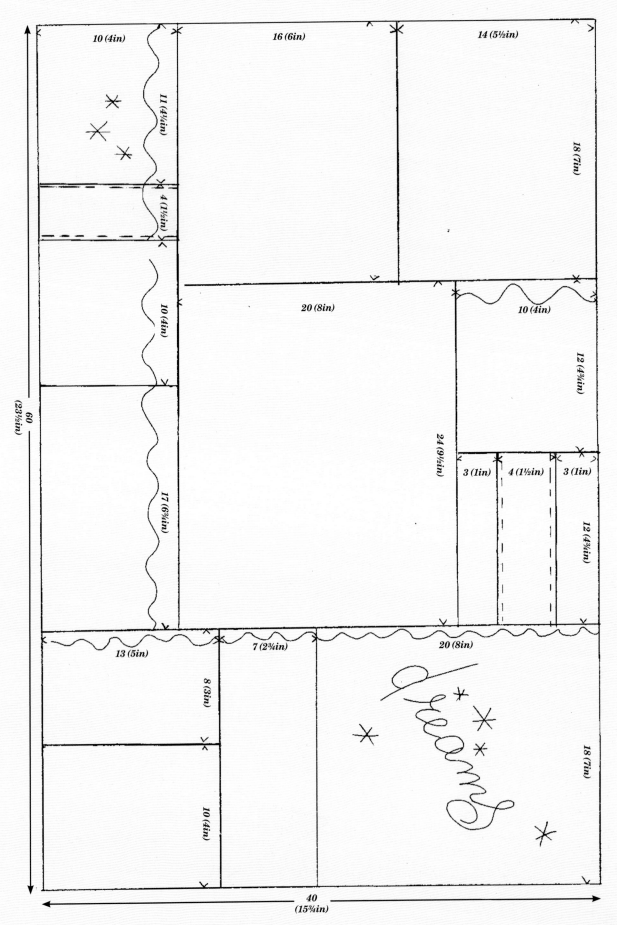

10 (4in)

16 (6in)

14 (5½in)

11 (4¼in)

18 (7in)

4 (1½in)

10 (4in)

20 (8in)

10 (4in)

12 (4¾in)

60
(23½in)

24 (9½in)

3 (1in) 4 (1½in) 3 (1in)

17 (6¾in)

12 (4¾in)

13 (5in)

7 (2¾in)

20 (8in)

8 (3in)

dreams

10 (4in)

18 (7in)

40
(15¾in)

See page 25 for how to use templates

sweet pea snuggler

designed by Camille Roskelley

This girly baby quilt is made all the lovelier by the addition of a little ribbon and a softly scalloped border

The arrival of a baby is such an exciting time for crafters, as we can indulge our sweet tooth with sherbert pastels, fun motifs and frilly embellishments. It's important when making a baby quilt not to get carried away and end up with something that fits a king size bed! This quilt is just 42 x 42in, the perfect size for a cot, or hung on the nursery wall as shown here.

All of the patchwork involved in Sweet Pea Snuggler is actually super-simple, and the last few touches add the final feminine look. Whether you decide to add the ribbon and scalloped border is entirely up to you – it's as sweet as pie either way!

Beginners will love the simple patchwork

DEEP SCARLET RED *and contemporary graphic patterned fabrics add a bit of an edge to what could otherwise be a sickly sweet palette.*

Cot-sized quilts also make gorgeous wall hangings – just slipstitch a simple sleeve to the backing and slide through a net curtain pole or dowelling to hang.

CUTTING

1 Divide your 64 5 x 5in squares into 32 pairs. Each pair is one set. In each set, place one square on top of the other, right sides up.

2 Cut each set of squares into two strips 2¼ x 5in, two strips 1½ x 5in, and two strips 1¼ x 5in.

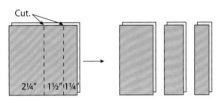

Cut.

2¼" 1½" 1¼"

3 Lay out the strips and then swap the center 1½in strips in each combination.

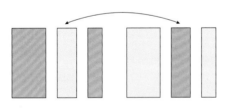

BLOCK ASSEMBLY

These super-simple blocks are each composed of three strips.

Note: All sewing is right sides together with a ¼in seam allowance, unless otherwise noted.

4 Sew each block together as follows: sew the 2¼in strip to the 1½in strip and then to the 1¼in strip. Press. You now have a block that measures 4 x 5in. Trim it to measure 4 x 4in.

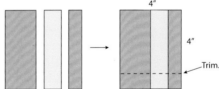

4"

4"

Trim.

5 Repeat the above steps to make a total of 64 blocks.

QUILT TOP ASSEMBLY

6 Sew the blocks in eight rows of eight, alternating the orientation of the blocks so they are random. Pin and sew the rows together to make the quilt top.

7 To make the ribbon embellishment, cut a 9in-long piece of ribbon and a 2½in-long piece of ribbon. For the bow, mark the center of the 9in piece and fold each end under toward the center, overlapping at the center by ¼in. Pin. Fold ribbon toward center and overlap by ¼in.

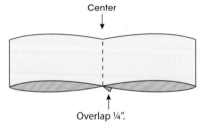

Center

Overlap ¼".

8 Pin and sew the remaining ribbon to the quilt top, overlapping rows 7 and 8. Topstitch by machine along each edge of the ribbon right across the quilt top. Wrap the 2½in piece of ribbon around the center of the bow and pin where desired. Topstitch around the 'knot'.

9 For the narrow inner borders: from the white border fabric, cut three strips 1½in x WOF. Measure the sides of the quilt top and measure two border strips the same length. Mark the border strips with a pin. Pin and stitch these border strips in place. Trim. Sew the two trimmed border pieces to the remaining border strip and cut the strip in half crosswise. As before, measure the correct lengths and sew the borders to the top and bottom of the quilt top. Make sure the corners are square.

10 For the middle border cut four strips 2¼in x WOF from the aqua border fabric. As before, measure the sides of the quilt top and measure two border strips the same length. Mark the border strips with a pin. Pin and stitch these border strips in place. Trim. Repeat to add the top and bottom borders. Make sure that the corners are square.

11 From the remaining white fabric, cut four strips 4½in x WOF. As before, measure the sides of the quilt top and measure two border strips the same length. Mark the border strips with a pin. Pin and stitch them in place. Trim. Repeat to add the top and bottom borders. Make sure the corners are square. »

This is a baby quilt that mom will cherish for years, and is sure to become a much-loved family heirloom

The bow is made using ice-blue cotton grosgrain ribbon for a modern finish.

Try adding a bow like this to other quilts and patchwork projects – so cute!

Pages 40–45:
This project and all associated text, images and patterns are taken from *Simplify with Camille Roskelley*, **published by Stash Books.**

SWEET PEA SNUGGLER
Templates – enlarge by 200%

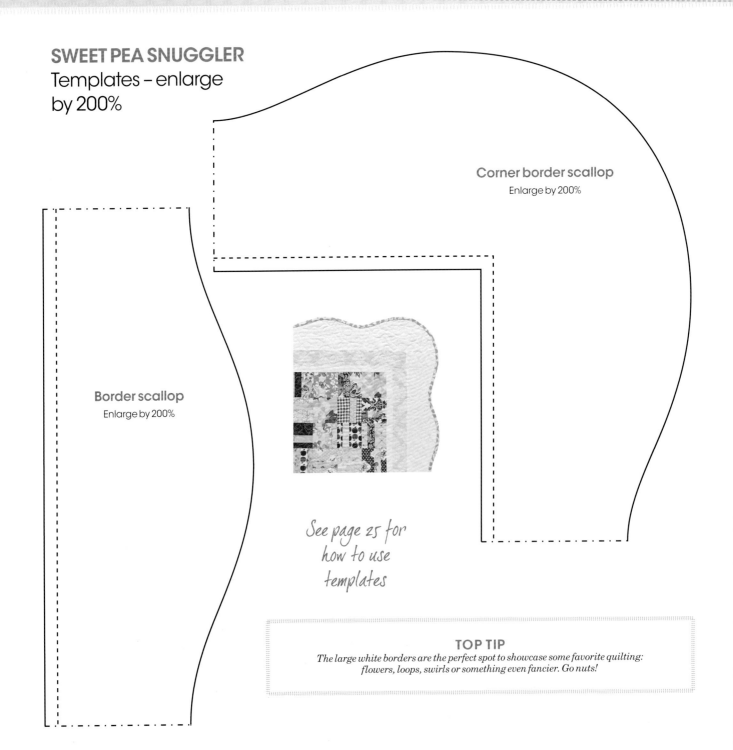

Corner border scallop
Enlarge by 200%

Border scallop
Enlarge by 200%

See page 25 for how to use templates

TOP TIP
The large white borders are the perfect spot to showcase some favorite quilting: flowers, loops, swirls or something even fancier. Go nuts!

MAKING THE SCALLOPS

12 Enlarge and trace the scallop pieces from the templates onto a piece of paper (see page 25). (You'll need eight Sweet Pea border scallop patterns and four corner border scallop patterns.) Cut out the pieces. Place a corner scallop piece on one corner of the quilt top, lining up the border lines with your middle border. Line up the other scallop pieces until you reach the next corner.

You may have to adjust slightly, as your quilt top may be a slightly different size. Continue placing the paper pieces all around the quilt top, adjusting as needed. Use a water-soluble fabric pen to trace the outer scallop shapes onto the outer white borders. Do not cut along the traced line until after the quilt is quilted and you are ready to apply the binding.

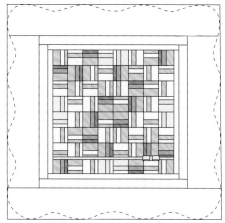

If you don't fancy making the scallop edge, this design would look equally beautiful with simple straight edges.

FINISHING

13 Make a quilt sandwich (see page 24) and machine or hand quilt as desired. Trim along the traced scallop line. Note that in this case the backing is a little smaller than usual, but why waste fabric? If your back is just a bit smaller than your quilt top, scoot your scallop a bit toward the center. The best part? No waste!

14 For the binding, cut 2½in strips on the bias at a 45 degree angle until you have 5½ yards of binding and join into one continuous strip. Continue as instructed in Binding, page 24, to sew on the binding. For this quilt, gently ease the binding around the curves as you stitch it to the quilt front and tuck as necessary on the inner angles when you turn it to the back.

Special handmade placemats add homespun charm to your dining table, especially if you make each one in a different colorway for an eclectic, fun effect.

scandi-style mats

designed by Chloë Owens

YOU WILL NEED

☐ Fabrics and felts

☐ Fusible interfacing

☐ Iron

☐ Fading fabric marker

☐ Ruler

☐ Sewing machine with embroidery foot

☐ Sewing threads to tone with fabrics and felts

☐ Heat-proof batting (wadding)

☐ Template on page 48

☐ Fabric glue (optional)

☐ Basic sewing kit (see page 16)

CUT OUT

☐ *Read the instructions carefully before cutting out what you need*

Impress your guests with a touch of Scandi style – they'll never guess how easy these were to make!

Brighten up dinnertime with these sweet Scandinavian-inspired placemats. The combination of patterned fabric and block color felt makes the appliqué stand out, while the simply curving machine stitch adds a delicate touch to the graphic shapes.

Appliqué is a simple yet effective technique that can be used on its own, or to embellish patchwork. Add as many or as few of the decorative shapes as you like as you build your confidence.

Simple shapes make appliqué a breeze!

TRY MIXING COOL *toned fabric with warm-toned felt and vice versa to ensure the appliqué 'pops' from the placemat!*

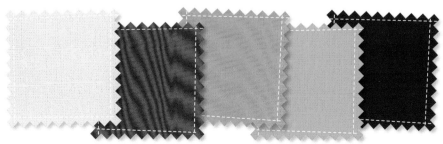

SCANDI-STYLE MATS
Template – enlarge by 200%

*Go to page 25 for how
to use the template*

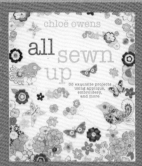

Pages 46–49:
This project and all associated text, images and patterns are taken from *All Sewn Up* by Chloë Owens, published by CICO Books. Visit **www.cicobooks.com**

1 Choose a background fabric: you will need two pieces measuring 15 x 15in (37 x 37cm) for each placemat. Then choose a selection of colored felts that complement the background fabric.

2 Iron fusible interfacing (see page 25) onto the wrong side of the front fabric. With the fabric marker and ruler, draw a line down the center. Enlarge the template by 200% and place the dotted line on the drawn line. Draw the swirls and leaves, then flip the template and draw them on the other side of the line. Using a decorative machine stitch, sew the center line. Then lower the feed dogs and free-machine embroider (see page 26) the swirls and leaves.

TOP TIP
Don't worry if your machine embroidery goes a bit freestyle – that spontaneity is what makes your creations so special!

3 Cut out all the birds, hearts and flowers from felt and glue or pin them symmetrically on the fabric. Using co-ordinating threads and straight stitch, free-machine embroider around each element.

4 Cut a piece of batting 14.5 x 14.5in (36 x 36cm). Put the two pieces of fabric right sides together and lay the batting on top. Pin, then sew around the edges, taking a ½in (1cm) seam allowance and leaving a 5in (13cm) gap.

5 Trim the corners without snipping into the stitching (see right). Turn right side out and press, pressing under the seam allowances across the gap, then topstitch (see tip box above right) around the mat with a contrast thread.

TIP TOP TOPSTITCHING

Topstitching not only firmly anchors your appliqué in place, but also adds definition to the edges for a crisp finish. It can be tricky, but like most things, practice makes perfect!

• You will sew a line of straight stitch very close to the edge of the project, about ⅛in (2mm) in from the edge is ideal.

• The trick is to position the fabric under the needle and lower the needle into the fabric to check it'll be sewing in the right place.

• Then, if there isn't a mark on the sewing machine's throat plate in the right place, stick a piece of masking tape to the plate at the edge of the fabric. Keep the edge of the fabric against the tape as you sew and your topstitching will look great.

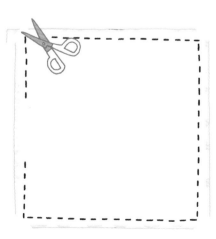

A design like this makes using up random fabric scraps a breeze. The mismatching of color and pattern becomes a creative feature and makes a true patchwork quilt.

big bold blocks! ♡

designed by Nicki Trench

Reduce the overall size of the quilt to make a colorful wall-hanging for a living room or play room

Bold colors give this quilt a wonderful scrappy, fun feel, with no two blocks alike. A truly unique item!

While the traditional 'log cabin' style has been used for this design, (using 'logs' of fabric to build a cabin around the central hearth, represented by the middle squares) the fabric selection is totally random. The result is a quilt that beginners will find great fun to make – just choose the colors and go!

The quilt is made up of a total of 30 blocks, each measuring about 12in (30cm) square when the quilt is completed. If you find you're pushed for time in which to fit your sewing, tackle this project one block at a time. You'll enjoy watching your pile of fabric disappear as the pile of blocks grows!

You might want to wait until you've finished the quilt top before you choose the binding fabric, to see which color from the blocks jumps out as the one you want to frame the whole design.

An easy way to play with bright colors!

BOLD INTENSE COLORS *can look great mixed together, especially when they are all the same brightness. The key is to be brave and don't be swayed from your path!*

Pages 50–53:
This project and all associated text, images and patterns are taken from ***A Passion for Quilting*** by Nicki Trench, published by CICO Books. Visit www.cicobooks.com

1 Press the fabrics for the patchwork. Cut strips of fabric 2in (5cm) wide. These will be added from the center outward to make the block, so will range in length from 2in (5cm) at the center to 12½in (32cm) at the outer edges. Decide roughly on the arrangement of the strips in the block.

2 Take one of the fabrics that will be at the center of the block and cut across it at right angles to a length of 2in (5cm), giving a 2in (5cm) square. Cut the second center square in a different fabric in the same way.

3 Pin the two squares right sides together and, using a ¼in (6mm) foot on your sewing machine, join them on one side with a ¼in (6mm) seam. Press the seam open.

4 Pin another length of fabric right sides together along one long edge of the pressed unit and attach it in the same way. Trim the edge level with the first pressed unit after sewing. Press the seam open.

5 Attach another strip across the two pieces just joined. Again, trim the edge level after sewing and press the seam open.

6 Keep adding strips in the order shown in the diagram. Remember to press the seam open each time you add a strip, and measure the total width of the piece periodically to ensure that the seams are accurate.

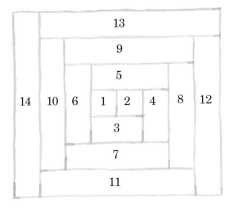

7 When you have added the final strip, press the block, place it on the cutting mat, and trim to 12½in (32cm) square.

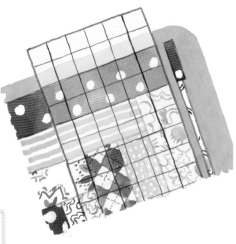

TOP TIP

Spray starch, available from the laundry section of the supermarket, is brilliant for taming small pieces of fabric. Spray it onto your fabric and press, and you'll find that even the tiniest pieces become a little rigid and so much easier to handle and sew.

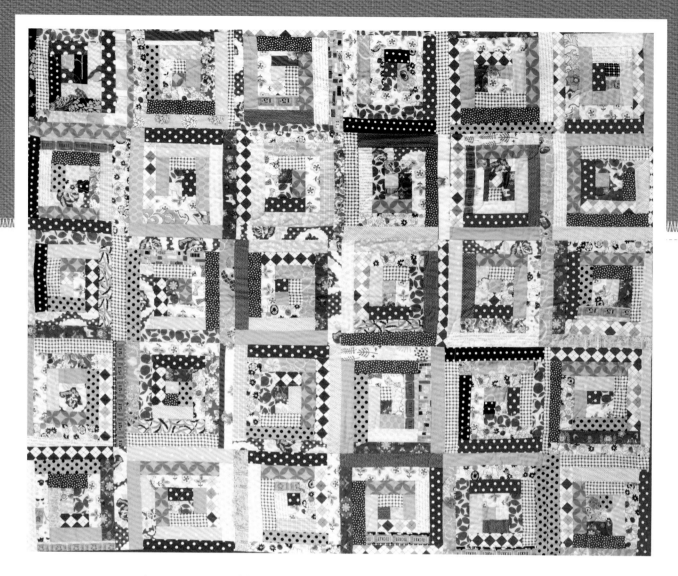

Imagine using this quilt as a playmat for the kids, or as a picnic rug for friends and family. The happy-go-lucky shapes and colors would add fun to any downtime!

8 Repeat steps 1 to 5 to make 30 log cabin blocks in the same way. Arrange the blocks in six rows of five blocks each. Sew the blocks together in horizontal rows, pressing the seams open each time, then sew the rows together to complete the quilt top. Press the quilt top well on the right side of the fabric.

9 Assemble the three layers of the quilt 'sandwich' (see page 24). Using curved safety pins and starting in the center of the quilt and working outward, pin through all layers to secure well, smoothing the quilt as you go.

10 Using a walking foot on your machine, if you have one, and a light-colored thread, start at one corner of the quilt and sew a meandering (curving) line with wide twists diagonally across the quilt. The stitching should pass through the corner of each block. When the first diagonal row is completed, repeat for each diagonal row in one direction.

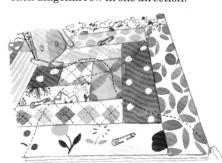

11 Starting from the opposite corner, repeat the process, making sure the quilt is smooth and unpuckered when one line of quilt stitching crosses another. This is best done by smoothing with both hands while sewing and is important on a large quilt. Trim the backing fabric and batting (wadding) level with the quilt top if necessary.

12 Cut strips of binding fabric on the straight grain, 2½in (6.5cm) wide. You will need two strips measuring the same as the top of the quilt, and two measuring the same as the sides plus 1in (2.5cm). Bind the quilt, using the method described on page 24.

Impress family and friends with the Blooming Chic throw, the ultimate snuggly blanket for your sofa!

blooming chic throw

designed by Sarah Fielke

YOU WILL NEED

- ☐ 10cm (4in) each of eight different light blue and eight different dark blue fabrics

- ☐ 10cm (4in) each of eight different light green and eight different dark green fabrics

- ☐ 10cm (4in) each of eight light orange or yellow and eight dark orange or yellow fabrics

- ☐ 10cm (4in) each of eight different light pink or red and eight dark pink or red fabrics

- ☐ 50cm (20in) dark brown fabric for accent squares

- ☐ 10cm (4in) medium floral fabric for border inserts

- ☐ 90cm (1yd) large floral fabric for border

- ☐ 70cm (27in) striped fabric for binding

- ☐ 4.2m (4⅝yd) backing fabric

- ☐ 210cm (83in) square cotton batting

- ☐ Basic sewing kit (page 16)

- ☐ Seam allowance: 6mm (¼in)

- ☐ Finished size:189cm (74½in) square

continued on page 56 »

This is one of those quilts that looks impressive yet is simple to make – all you need is patience!

Flowers bloom and leaves sway in the lush botanical gardens of this quilt. Imagine snuggling up under this on the sofa on a chilly evening – you can almost smell the heady scent! Large-scale floral prints and co-ordinating graphics are the secret to making your own garden bloom. Be sure to include a wide variety of prints, but make certain that the pairs of fabrics you choose are complementing each other, not contrasting, and you will create a blended garden bed just like the one shown here.

The Blooming Chic throw might not be your first choice of project if you're new to patchwork, but it's much easier than it looks, being about organization and patience rather than technical acrobatics! Once you've got a few of the smaller projects under your belt, you may well come back to this project – it's well worth it.

A good challenge for confident beginners!

CHOOSE YOUR PRINTS *after you've read the materials list and looked at the image of the complete quilt on page 57 to decide the look you want to achieve.*

» CUT OUT

All fabrics are strip-cut across the width of the fabric from fold to selvedge unless otherwise specified or unless you are using a directional print

From each of the 10cm (4in) of light and dark fabric pieces cut:
One strip, 3⅞in wide, across the width of the fabric, giving a total of 64 strips. Separate the fabrics into 32 pairs, each containing a light and a dark strip from the same colorway (eight pairs of each colorway)

From each colorway pair cut:
Two pairs of squares, each 3⅞in (four squares in total). Cross-cut these pairs of squares on one diagonal into four pairs of half-square triangles (eight half-square triangles in total). Trim the remaining section of each colorway pair to be 3½in wide

From each trimmed pair cut:
Six pairs of squares, each 3½in (12 squares in total). Set the eight half-square triangles and 12 squares from each colorway pair aside in their pairs (zip-lock bags are handy here for keeping things in order) and continue with the remaining fabric pairs until you have cut all the squares and triangles for 32 pairs

continued on page 58 »

CONSTRUCTING THE QUILT TOP

1 Using the photograph of the finished quilt on the opposite page and the block diagram below, begin by laying out the pieces for each row. Your quilt should be 21 squares across each row and 21 rows down.

Each block of the quilt contains the four pairs of half-triangles and the six pairs of squares that you cut from a light/dark colorway pair, as well as four brown accent squares. However, the quilt top is constructed square by square, and row by row, rather than a block at a time.

As you lay out the rows, you will see how the blocks in each colorway are formed and it helps to visualize the design in terms of blocks.

2 You will also see from the photograph that the edges of the patchworked quilt top are composed of half-blocks and, in the upper right-hand and lower left-hand corners, of quarter-blocks. For these rows, you will need to divide some of your sets of square and triangle pairs into the appropriate number.

3 When happy with the arrangement of squares, sew the first row together into a strip. When you come to the half-square triangles, sew the triangles together into a square (Diagram 1). Press the seam allowance toward the darker fabric, trim off the 'ears' at each corner and then sew the completed square to the strip, and continue. Press all the seams toward » the dark fabrics.

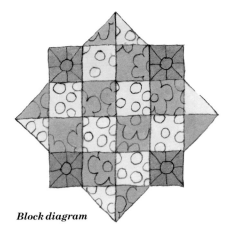

Block diagram

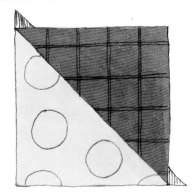

Diagram 1

TOP TIP
Follow the layout of alternating colors as in the picture, but don't be too worried about where each fabric goes yet. It is much better to lay the fabric down, and then move the colors around until you are happy with the layout.

Include a wide variety of prints, but make certain that the pairs of fabrics you choose are complementing each other, not contrasting, and you will create a blended garden bed just like the one shown here

Quilting
from little things...

best-selling author
Sarah Fielke

Pages 54–59:
This project and all associated text, images and patterns are taken from *Quilting From Little Things* by Sarah Fielke, published by Murdoch Books. Visit www.murdochbooks.co.uk

» **From dark-brown fabric cut:**
Five strips, 3½in wide. Cross-cut these strips into 3½in squares – you will need 49 squares in all

From border insert fabric cut:
One strip, 3½in wide. From this strip, cross-cut seven pieces, each 6 x 3½in

From border floral cut:
Six strips, 6in wide

From red binding fabric cut:
Nine strips, 3in wide. Set aside for binding

QUILTING
If you are new to patchwork, you may prefer to use a long-arm quilting service to quilt your design.

4 Sew the second row. Press the seams toward the dark fabrics.

5 Continue in this way until you have completed all 21 rows of the quilt top. Now sew the first row to the second row, being careful to match the seams when the squares meet. Continue until you have sewn all 21 rows together. Press the top carefully and make sure that it is square.

BORDER

6 Beginning and ending with a 6in border insert piece, sew the seven inset pieces and six floral border strips together, end to end, into one long strip.

7 Measure your quilt through the center in both directions to get the true width. It should measure 63½in. (If it does not, you should adjust the following border measurements accordingly to match.)

8 Cut two strips from the assembled border fabric, each 63½in long. Find the center of one edge of the quilt and the center of one border strip and pin, then pin the ends together. Pin in between, easing if needed. Sew and repeat with the opposite border. Press.

9 Measure the quilt across the middle again with the borders attached. Cut the remaining two borders to this measurement. Attach the remaining two borders as above. Your quilt top is now complete!

BACKING, QUILTING AND BINDING
Cut the backing fabric in half crosswise, giving two pieces, each 210cm (83in) long. Trim the selvedges and sew the pieces together along the length to form one backing piece. Press the seam allowance open.

Refer to pages 23–26 for instructions on finishing.

The squares of dark brown that sit around the block edges add just enough definition with their darker color. The yellow pattern means that they're still softer than a solid color

This is a brilliant 'stash buster' project! Only a small amount of each fabric is required, so raid your fabric stash and start using up all those odds and ends!

This bag is actually made from four cotton tea towels, always a great source of new fabric in smaller quantities!

fast favorite tote

designed by Cath Kidston

YOU WILL NEED

- ☐ 140 x 70cm (1½yd x 27½in) spot print fabric

- ☐ 140 x 40cm (1½yd x 15¾in) floral print fabric

- ☐ Stranded embroidery thread in red

- ☐ Basic sewing kit (see page 16)

- ☐ Seam allowance: 1cm (½in)

CUT OUT

From spot print fabric:
- ☐ Seventeen 12cm (4¾in) squares

- ☐ Two 52 x 32cm (20½ x 12½in) lining panels

- ☐ One 42 x 12cm (16½ x 4¾in) lining base

From floral print fabric:
- ☐ Seventeen 12cm (4¾in) squares

- ☐ One 22 x 12cm (8¾ x 4¾in) pocket

- ☐ Two 60 x 8cm (23½ x 3in) handle strips

There's always room in your life for a new bag, and one as pretty and practical as this will become a favorite!

Bags are a great way to show off your patchwork and sewing skills to the outside world, and ensure that your hard work pays you back with admiring glances and comments!

Make just one tote, or a couple to suit different looks or occasions. The bag shown here is made from robust cotton that will look and wear like your favorite denim jeans or jacket. Made from a sturdy fabric, this style of bag could also be popped in the corner of the kitchen to collect paper recycling or cans, then easily carried to the recycling center.

Alternatively, make it from lightweight cottons, linen, satins or a mix of similar weight fabrics to produce a stylish and useful one-of-a-kind tote.

Great for confident beginners

DUSKY VINTAGE SHADES *are a great choice as they look better the more the fabric is used. Here the blues and pinks are sprinkled with white, cream and flashes of red – a true classic.*

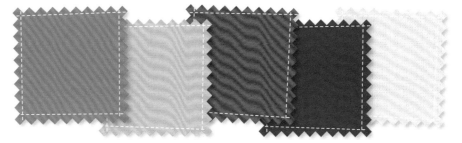

Pages 60–63: This project and all associated text, images and patterns taken from *Patch!* by **Cath Kidston**, published by **Quadrille**. **Photos © Pia Tryde**

1 Lay out the 30 squares that make up the main bag in a checkerboard pattern, in three horizontal rows of ten. Sew them together in vertical rows of three, with right sides facing.

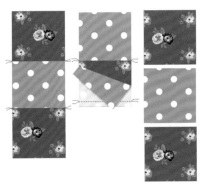

2 Press the seam allowances in opposite directions so that they will lie flat when the rows are joined. For each row with a spot square at the top and bottom, press the seams downwards and for each row with a floral square at the top and bottom, press the seams upwards.

3 Join the rows together to make a long rectangle. With right sides facing, match the long edges so that the seams butt up against each other. Insert a pin at each seam line and at the top and bottom corners, then machine stitch.

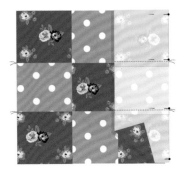

4 Press all the vertical seams open. Seam and press the two side edges to make a cylinder of patchwork. Press.

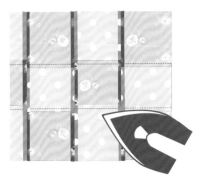

5 Sew the remaining four squares together to make the base, alternating the spot and floral prints. Press the seams open.

6 With right sides facing inwards, pin one long edge of the bag base to four squares along the bottom edge of the main bag, matching the open seams. Pin the other long edge to the opposite side of the bag, leaving the short edges open. Make a 5mm snip into the bottom of each corner seam to open out the allowance. Machine stitch these two seams, starting and finishing each line of stitching 1cm from the short edge and working a few backwards stitches to strengthen.

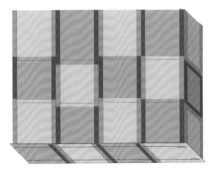

7 Pin the short edges of the base to the bag and machine stitch. Work two more rounds of stitching over the first lines to reinforce the seam.

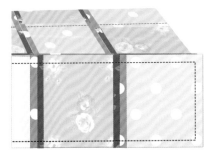

8 Using a thick crewel needle and three strands of red embroidery thread, work a line of running stitch, 5mm in from each side seam.

9 Neaten the top edge of the pocket with a narrow double hem. Press under a 1cm (½in) turning along the other three sides. Pin the pocket to one lining panel, 6cm (2½in) down from the top edge and 11cm (4¼in) in from the left side edge. Machine down in place, working a few extra stitches at the beginning and end of the seam.

10 With right sides facing, join the two edges of the lining panels to make a cylinder. Press the seams open, then press back a 15mm (⅝in) turning around the top edge. Make a 6mm (¼in) snip into the seam allowance on the bag at each corner as for the main bag. With right sides facing, pin on the lining base, lining up two opposite corners to the two seams. Sew in place with two rounds of stitching.

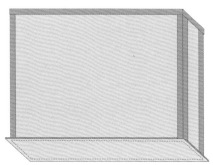

11 Slip the lining inside the bag, matching up the base and two side edge seams. Pin together around the opening - the lining should sit about 5mm (⅛in) down from the top edge of the bag. Machine stitch 3mm from the top edge of the lining.

Embellish other parts of the bag using the same simple top stitch in a contrasting color.

12 Press each handle strip in half width ways and unfold. Press a 1cm turning each of the four edges, then re-press the center crease. Machine stitch 3mm (³⁄₁₆in) from each long edge. Tack the ends of the handles to the sides of the bag so that they lie 5cm (2in) down from the top edge and overlap the side patchwork seams. Sew down with rectangles of reinforcing stitch.

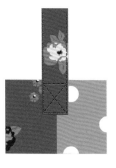

quirky message board

designed by Katrien Van Deuren

Cork noticeboards are so last year. Make this one and see how much less forgetful you'll become!

SIMPLE RUSTIC COLORS *such as the natural linen used here make the perfect backdrop for colored bunting and pegs.*

What could be nicer than an adorable noticeboard for your kitchen made using an embroidery hoop? Maybe a board with tiny colorful bunting and clothes pegs, of course! This project can be made using any sized hoop, which is easy to find in needlework and sewing shops. The bunting is very simple to stitch, as it's all straight lines in nice bite-size chunks.

This is a great project for odds and ends of fabric, string and pegs – you've probably got everything you need lurking at the back of the kitchen drawer!

The perfect quick gift!

TOP TIP
You can buy painted pegs, but painting them yourself is very easy. Try painting them multicolored like these ones, or use a single color for a subtle finish.

Be back soon!

STITCH THE APPLIQUÉ

1 Iron the fusible fleece, following the manufacturer's directions, to the back of the linen fabric.

2 Arrange the triangles to create two rows of garlands on the linen. Pin in place and sew the triangles onto the linen by machine, using black thread. First sew a straight line across the whole length of the garland row, starting and stopping at least 2in past the end of the string of garlands to make the end of the string 'disappear' under the hoop after framing. Then stitch around the triangles, following the V-shaped outline.

bright ideas!

For a **simple picture**, stitch lines of bunting all the way down and frame in the same way

Colored felt also works for this project

Hold that thought! The adorable bunting and colorful pegs on this crafty noticeboard make it fun for everyone in the house to leave quick messages and notes.

Hang your hoop using ribbon, as shown here, or more of the brown twine. Look out for colorful baker's twine too

3 Optional: add a small bow at the end of one (or both) of the garlands, using a free-motion machine embroidery technique (see page 26). Alternatively, embroider the bow by hand.

ASSEMBLE THE BOARD

4 Arrange thick string across the linen base to form a 'clothes line' underneath the garlands.

5 Center the linen piece in the wooden embroidery hoop and smooth the surface by pulling gently at the excess fabric. Tighten the hoop with the screw.

6 Trim the excess fabric and fusible fleece into a circle around the hoop, leaving a 2in allowance for gluing.

7 Carefully peel the fusible fleece from the 2in allowance of fabric. Cut away this excess fusible fleece to reduce the bulk and fold the 2in allowance over the hoop toward the back and glue in place.

TO FINISH

Glue the felt circle to the back of the hoop. Use thick string to tie a little bow at the end of the clothes line and attach the wooden pegs.

Leave a message!

Pages 64–65: This project and all associated text and patterns are taken from *Zakka Style* compiled by **Rashida Coleman-Hale**, published by **Stash Books**.

A chair cover like this
will look just as good
fluttering in the summer
breeze on a garden seat
as it will covering a
chair in a cozy kitchen

*Pretty faded florals and simple lines
are typical Scandinavian style, and
turn an ordinary chair into a truly
special one-off creation.*

vintage floral seat

designed by Clare Youngs

YOU WILL NEED

- ☐ Selection of patterned handkerchiefs

- ☐ 16–20in (40–50cm) ribbon, ½in (1cm) wide

- ☐ 8–10 buttons

- ☐ Basic sewing kit (see page 16)

- ☐ Seam allowance: ½in (1cm) and ¼in (5mm) – check instructions for where to use

CUT OUT

Unlike other patchwork designs, which require accurate joining together of same-size fabric pieces, this project requires a more relaxed approach

As you'll find when reading the project instructions, you will need to lay your handkerchiefs out on the floor and have a play with them until you decide on your layout

Some may then need trimming to fit your intended design, but the exact measurements will depend on the size of the chair that you are covering

You can patchwork with most fabrics, such as the vintage handkerchiefs used to cover this little seat!

aking a slipcover is a great way to give an old chair a brand new lease of life, but why stick to conventional fabric when there is so much else out there to play with?

Look out for old linen tea towels or embroidered tray cloths and napkins in charity shops, and at yard sales. You may even have a few lurking at the back of the kitchen cupboard! This slipcover is made from vintage handkerchiefs and will add a country vibe to any interior. Although the handkerchiefs are pretty in their own right, combining them creates something extra special.

It's so simple to upcycle!

FADED VINTAGE PASTELS *mixed and matched is the key to this color scheme – keep your fabric choices soft and worn looking.*

Pages 66–69:
This project and all associated text, images and patterns are taken from *Scandinavian Needlecraft* by Clare Youngs, published by CICO Books. Visit **www.cicobooks.com**

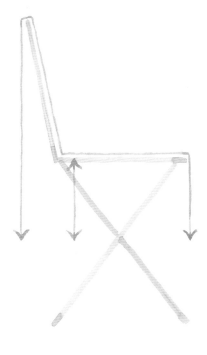

1 First, measure your chair. The cover consists of one long piece that covers the legs, seat and back, and two side pieces. Start with the long piece. Work out how far down the front legs you want the cover to extend, then measure up from that point, across the seat, up the back, and down the other side to the same level as on the front. Then work out the depth of the two side panels to match.

2 Lay the handkerchiefs on the floor and move them around until you're happy with the layout. You may need to cut them to get the right width and length – or simply to break the patchwork up into less regular shapes.

3 Make the long piece first. The panel should be larger than you need, so that you can trim and hem it to the right size. Pin the fabrics right sides together and machine stitch, leaving ¼in (5mm) seam allowances. Press the seams open. Trim the panel to size, leaving a ½in (1cm) seam allowance all the way around. Turn over a double ¼in (5mm) hem all around, pin, and machine stitch.

4 Make the two side panels in the same way, again leaving a ½in (1cm) seam allowance all the way around. If necessary, turn over a double ¼in (5mm) hem around one long and both short sides of each side panel, pin, and machine stitch. (If you're using handkerchiefs the sides will already be hemmed of course.) Pin the fourth side under the main panel, and machine-stitch it in place, leaving a ½in (1cm) seam allowance.

If you're inspired to cover a set of chairs, make your flea-market finds go further. Using plain cotton for the back of the cover keeps your vintage fabrics on show, or cover seat cushions instead – the same look with less fabric

Text © Clare Youngs. Photographs © Loupe Images/Claire Richardson.
Artwork © Loupe Images/Kate Simunek.

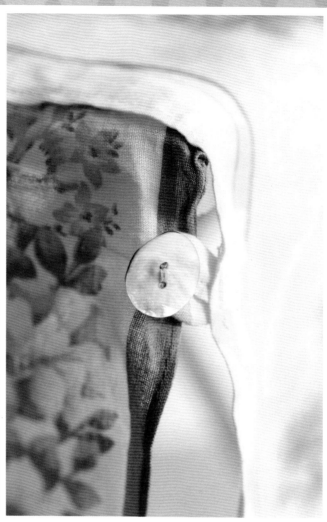

Shell and pearl buttons are perfect for this look, but you could use anything from your button tin. There's nothing more satisfying than finding a home for all those stray buttons!

5 Fold the ribbon in half widthwise, press, and machine-stitch along the raw, unfolded edge. Cut into 2in (5cm) sections and fold each one in half to make a loop. Pin the loops in position on the wrong side of the panels; you will need at least two on each side of the back section and one on each leg section. Sew a line of stitching across the bottom raw edges of the loop to secure. Sew buttons in position to complete. Press and then cover your chair!

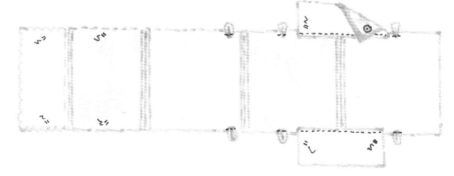

FINDING & USING VINTAGE FABRICS

Old fabric scraps are a dream come true for thrifty patchworkers. Pick up material from second-hand shops or upcycle household items to create new, yet unique designs

F abric is everywhere – the clothes we wear, the soft furnishings in our homes, not to mention the rolls and rolls of gorgeous fabrics available from the shops and online. But do you have to spend your hard-earned cash on new material to sew with? Of course not! We've got all the best ways to get fabric for free and turn it into something truly special. Why not get started right away and make something gorgeous today?

Vintage chic: Jo Grant (jogrant. wordpress.com) joined forces with her mom to create this amazing quilt (see full quilt, opposite) from a selection of vintage tea towels and tablecloths.

Look out for words and messages on tea towels – they're such fun to incorporate!

When on the hunt for fabrics, you don't have to rely on what you can find at home. Ask friends and family, rummage through charity shops (always great for curtains and table cloths), get online and scour Ebay, Freecycle and Gumtree, and never pass up the opportunity for a nosey round a yard sale or rummage sale. And remember, it's not the item you're interested in – it's the fabric. Try to see that patterned skirt from the '80s with dodgy-length hemline and hideous waistband as an unpicked piece of fabric and not something you'd never be seen dead in. Similarly, big curtains with an in-your-face pattern might be something you'd never want to hang at your window, but imagine a small square of the fabric mixed with calmer colors and you might be on to a winner.

CAN I REALLY MAKE PATCHWORK FROM…

TEA TOWELS
Yes! And in some ways the older the better, as the fabric will be lovely and soft. After washing and ironing, inspect carefully for stains and holes – and cut off unusable parts. If you're making a whole bag, quilt, cushion or other patchwork project from tea towels, try to use ones with similar fabric weight to help prevent your finished item getting misshapen.

VINTAGE SCARVES
Like tea towels, vintage scarves need to be carefully inspected for wear and tear.

Very fine silk can be difficult to sew, so it's best to stick to medium-weight scarves. You can use them whole, or cut them to create smaller shapes and then piece them together in a patchwork pattern of your choice!

CLOTHES
Before sending your unwanted clothes to the charity shop or recycling bank, have a good look at the fabric they're made from. Could you use it for patchwork? A shirt with a stain on the front might have a perfectly usable

back; and old-fashioned or no-longer-fits dress might have whole swathes of fabric you could re-purpose. Remember that you will find woven fabric is far easier to sew than the stretchy fabric of T-shirts and leggings.

TABLE LINEN
Tablecloths and napkins – especially vintage embroidered linen – can make the most beautiful patchwork. Damask is another prime candidate – with a subtle pattern woven into the fabric that only shows at certain angles. As with

Jo's stunning quilt was bordered and then backed with red damask for a luxury finish.

SHARON LLOYD, who owns her own online craft shop (visit www.folksy.com/shops/TheOldButton) – upcycled some old jeans and shirts to make this fab patchwork quilt.

"I recycled two pairs of faded old jeans and four old cotton checked shirts in lovely rich reds and denim blues, cutting as many squares as I could out of each garment. Each individual patch was made by sandwiching soft bamboo wadding between a denim and checked square, then machine quilting. The quilted patches were sewn together in a checkerboard pattern with the raw edges on one side, creating a beautiful reversible quilt with a smooth side and a frayed side."

COST-EFFECTIVE PLACES TO SCORE GREAT FABRIC

- ♡ Charity shops
- ♡ Online
- ♡ Friends and family
- ♡ Yard sales
- ♡ Junk shops
- ♡ Cupboards and boxes at home
- ♡ Fabric shop remnants bin

tea towels, inspect carefully and cut out any stained or worn areas before you start. You don't want to notice the ghost of a gravy splodge after finishing your patchwork quilt!

CURTAINS

Old curtains can be a great source of pattern and color. The fabric weight of curtains will tend to be heavier than more 'traditional' quilting fabrics, but as long as you create your patchwork designs from fabrics of similar weight your results will be stunning.

Simply cut off any header tape and remove the lining, then decide how to piece your old curtains together! Keep an eye out for washing instructions too – you'll find many curtain fabrics are dry-clean only.

MIX AND MATCH

The joy of patchwork is being able to mix together different fabric colors and patterns to create your very own design. It's even more joyous if at the same time you know you're recycling – but when you aren't just picking out the latest range of quilting fabric from your fave fabric shop there are a few things you need to bear in mind.

There are loads of different types of fabric, and they don't all behave in the same way when they're washed. If you combine patches of light summery cotton with patches of heavy damask curtain fabric, you'll probably end up with a quilt that looks great at first, but if you wash it might get a bit out of shape. Similarly, patches of a cotton tablecloth sewn together with patches of a '70s polyester dress could look a little bit odd once quilted and washed: the cotton will shrink and crumple a little bit but the polyester will remain resolutely straight, firm and shiny.

The safest way to proceed is only combine fabrics of similar weights and made of the same fibers (i.e. cottons with cottons, polyester with polyester etc.), or do some test patches to make sure that the effects created by mixing fibers and weights are what you want to achieve.

PREPARING FABRIC FOR UPCYCLING

If you're re-purposing fabric, you need to prepare it properly for making into patchwork. It doesn't need to take long, and in most cases your washing machine and scissors will do most of the work for you!

1 Wash fabrics according to the washing instructions on the original garment, cushion cover, curtain… you get the idea. If in doubt, dry clean (if you don't mind having a dry-clean-only quilt) or machine wash on your machine's gentlest, coolest wash and spin cycles.

2 Once dried, spread the item out and undo seams, cut off waistbands, cut out zips, collars, header bands on curtains – and preserve the largest possible areas of flat fabric.

3 Iron your flat fabric carefully, cutting away any holes, stains or other fabric 'blemishes'.

The faded colors of this
quilt have a soothing,
relaxing effect, making this
color scheme perfect if you
want to create a special
corner of the house to call
your own, such as
a study or craft room

**Quilts aren't just for beds!
Try draping one over a table
for an unexpected pop of
color and comfort.**

ice-cream quilt

designed by Jane Brocket

YOU WILL NEED

Quilt top:
Gather a mix of ½yd/m and ¼yd/m pieces and smaller offcuts or cherished scraps, to make up a minimum of 4½yd/m. I prefer not to begin with a set yardage; instead I simply gather what I have and do not worry about the possibility of leftovers. So I would always start with more than 4½yd/m and then use what is needed. Ten to twelve fabrics will be enough to give a good variety and a few more could enhance the mix

See page 74 for Jane's guidance when choosing your fabric

Backing:
You will also need 4½yd/m of fabric for the backing (this gives enough allowance for a large-scale repeat like the ones I have used)

The binding for a quilt this size takes 17½in (44.5cm) of fabric

continued on page 74 »

Choosing fabric isn't a science, as Jane Brocket proves in this wonderfully freewheeling quilt

One of the joys of patchwork is mixing and matching, mixing and clashing, and mixing and experimenting with fabrics. The nature of patchwork means that your interpretation of a design will always be different from the next person. If you feel at all apprehensive about such a freeflow approach, turn to page 87 to read about Jane's own inspirations for this design. Her own enthusiasm and simple approach is sure to fire your imagination! Also look at our Creative Inspiration feature on pages 8–9, which will help you to discover your own sources of ideas from all around you.

Here Jane takes you through the process of how to make this show-stopping quilt for yourself…

Freestyle patchwork for beginners!

CAPTURE YOUR IDEAS *in color, such as these ice-cream sundae shades that make you think of a blissful stroll along the beach, complete with stripy deck chairs!*

Take your time when choosing fabrics and designing. Enjoy the experience and savor the chance to be truly creative!

» YOU WILL ALSO NEED

☐ A piece of wadding 3–4in (7.5–10cm) larger all around than the quilt top (I use 100% organic cotton with scrim)

☐ 100% cotton all-purpose sewing thread in ecru or taupe for the machine piecing

☐ 100%cotton quilting thread

☐ Seam allowance: all seam allowances are ¼in (6mm) unless otherwise specified

☐ Finished size: 56½ x 72½in (143.5 x 184cm)

CHOOSING FABRIC

1. Gather 12 to 20 fabrics if you want to make a quilt similar to mine in style (I used 17 in the Ice-Cream quilt), or fewer for a less variegated effect.

2. Play with them, making line-ups and changing the order frequently, as you may discover a fabric looks awful next to one fabric but great surrounded by others.

3. Do try what might appear to be no-go fabrics; it only takes a moment add a fabric, take a squint at it, and remove if necessary (I discarded two in the Candy version: a pink print that was too pale, and a yellow that stood out too much because it was too ochre).

4. On the other hand, you might discover a wonderful new combination that sets off the whole quilt. This is what happened when I introduced the pink and white spot and the huge 'Russian Rose' fabrics into the Ice-Cream version.

CUTTING OUT

1 Don't start by cutting out all your fabric at once. Instead, cut out a few strips from each of the possible fabrics and play with them. Once you know what does and does not work, cut out more. I cut out in three or four batches for each quilt, to avoid wastage of fabrics that did not turn out as well as expected.

2 All strips need to be cut to 2½ x 8½in (6 x 21.5cm) to make finished strips 2 x 8in (5 x 20cm), which then make each finished square 8 x 8in (20 x 20cm). Cut out up to four strips at a time by folding the fabric in half selvedge to selvedge, then in half again, and then cutting with a rotary cutter and ruler.

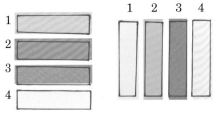

Strips for block 1 Strips for block 2

DESIGNING

3 Build up the quilt layout until you have the size you want and like (but remember to adjust the requirements for backing and binding fabrics and wadding if you are making it larger or smaller). Mine is seven squares across and nine squares down.

4 Stand back and appraise the quilt. Allow your eye to move over it, looking for problem areas. Do you have too many stand-out fabrics leaping out at you in the wrong places? Can you see fabrics repeated or too close together where you don't want them? Is there another fabric that could be introduced to enliven/ balance the effect?

5 Don't forget to change your vantage point so that you are looking critically from different angles. »

Top section of quilt – the quilt has seven blocks across and nine blocks down

The stripes of this design create a gorgeous basket weave effect – a classic design reinterpreted in beautiful bold prints!

Jane Brocket

The Gentle Art of
Quilt-Making

15 Projects Inspired by Everyday Beauty

Pages 72–77:
This project and all
associated text, images
and patterns are taken
from The Gentle Art
of Quilt-Making
by Jane Brocket,
published by
Collins & Brown.

SEWING

6 Once you are happy with the layout, you need to sew together each block. I do this by picking up the four strips in the correct order, taking them to the machine, sewing them, and returning the newly made square to its correct place in the layout. This is so I don't lose track of what goes where – something that is very easy to do.

7 If you don't have the time and space to leave the layout on the floor, you need to make a little pile of strips for each square and number it with a Post-It note pinned through the pile, so that you know where it belongs (for example, 'row 2, square 3').

The Ice-Cream quilt has a soothing sorbet color palette which sets the tone for this yummy design.

8 Once you have machine-pieced all the squares, it's time to iron them. Pick up the squares in columns or rows – I prefer to work in columns with this design (number the top square for each column or row and keep the pile together). Press all seams to one side, keeping the same direction on every square. So I ironed all horizontal stripe squares with the seams facing downwards, and all the vertical stripe squares with the seams facing to the right. Iron all the right sides, too.

9 Now sew the squares into strips, creating rows across or columns down and keeping them clearly numbered. Iron each strip, pressing the seams in alternating directions – odd rows facing up and even rows facing down, or vice versa.

10 Machine-piece the top with the strips of squares by sewing them together in the right order (it's only after this that you can discard the Post-It notes and pin numbering system, although I always leave the top left marker in until the binding has been attached). Iron again, this time pressing all the new seams in the same direction.

FINISHING

11 Make the backing by sewing together two widths of fabric with a ½in (1cm) seam, making sure that the back is 3–4in (7.5–10cm) larger all round than the quilt top. (You can trim the selvedges of the backing fabric if you like, but I don't bother.) Press the seam open.

12 Make the quilt sandwich and pin (see page 24 for more step-by-step information on how to make a quilt sandwich).

Quilt backing doesn't have to be boring – take a leaf from Jane's book and choose a suitably stunning print.

13 Hand-quilt with 100% cotton quilting thread. I used a pale, dusty pink thread on the Ice-Cream quilt (and sky blue on the Candy quilt, see opposite) to make a grid of running stitches. Follow horizontal and/or vertical seams and stitch lines ¼in (6mm) away from the seam. Alternatively, machine-quilt if you prefer.

14 Take the quilt to the beach with a flask of tea, a warm jumper and a good book! Or, if it's warm, sit on it while you eat seaside rock and ice-cream in the sun.

Sweet color selection:
Turn to page 87 to read
about Jane's inspiration
for the Candy quilt colors.

Planning your own color combination usually means coming up with more than one option at first. So why make one quilt when you can make two! This is Jane's alternative to the Ice-Cream quilt – Candy. Delicious!

Depending on the fabric you choose, this quilt would be perfect for a girl or a boy – anything from girly polka dots to khaki camouflage will complement the design.

fun with pattern!

designed by Kathy Doughty

YOU WILL NEED

☐ Four patterned feature panels, 47cm (18in) square prior to trimming, or fat quarters with an interesting pattern

☐ 2.5m (3yd) assorted light and 2.5m (3yd) assorted dark fabrics

☐ 90cm (36in) border fabric

☐ 5m (5½yd) backing fabric

☐ 60cm (24in) binding fabric (requirements are based on fabric 112cm/44 in wide)

☐ 1.7 x 2.5m (1¾ x 2¾yd) piece cotton wadding

☐ Basic sewing kit (see page 16)

☐ Seam allowance: ¼in

☐ Finished size: King single, 150 x 225cm (59 x 89in)

☐ Finished block size: 18½in square, inc. seam allowance

All fabrics are strip cut across the width of the fabric, from selvedge to fold (cut off all selvedges first). The following cutting instructions are labeled alphabetically, but cut the largest pieces first and use remaining fabric to cut the smaller strips

continued on page 80 »

Big print fabric can be hard to cut into, purely because you love the print so much! Here's a way to use it whole

Showcase big bold prints by mixing patterned fabric with simple patchwork blocks. This quilt is the perfect choice when you just can't bear to cut up an amazing print, or have a large print that just doesn't look right cut into little pieces. In this case, retro starburst fabric is the star of the show, but these blocks can feature any motif or pattern you choose – look for big graphics, big flowers or bold spots.

The patchwork squares in this quilt are worked in a traditional design known as Courthouse Steps – look for fabrics that include light and dark, and a variety of colors. The darker fabric will add definition to the Courthouse Steps. The placement of the light and dark fabrics varies within and between the blocks, giving a touch of randomness to the quilt's structure. All in all, with a little planning, you'll have a gloriously funky quilt!

Quick impact with minimal cutting!

DARK AND LIGHT *colors mixed together are needed to make certain designs sing out, so make sure you have a variety of each in your stash.*

Take your time and stay organized when cutting and preparing the fabric pieces. In fact, the whole process can be very therapeutic!

» CUT OUT

Block A

☐ Trim the four feature panels to 18½in square and set aside

Block B

☐ Cut all the Block B fabrics (the assorted light and dark fabrics) into 21in strips. Cut the longest pieces first and the smaller pieces from the remainders, as follows. It is helpful to build one block at a time and sew it together, then proceed to the next one

For each Block B

(cut 11 sets in this manner):
☐ Cut one 2½in square for the center (A)
☐ Cut two 2in contrast squares (B)
☐ Cut two light (C1) and two dark (C2) strips 6½in long
☐ Cut two light (D1) and two dark (D2) strips 10½in long
☐ Cut two light (E1) and two dark (E2) strips 14½in long
☐ Cut two light or dark strips 18½in long (F)

Borders and binding

☐ From the border fabric, cut five strips 6½in wide. Sew them end to end and cut in half widthways. Trim them to fit the five rows once they are assembled. Each border should be 90½in long

☐ From the binding fabric, cut eight strips 3in long

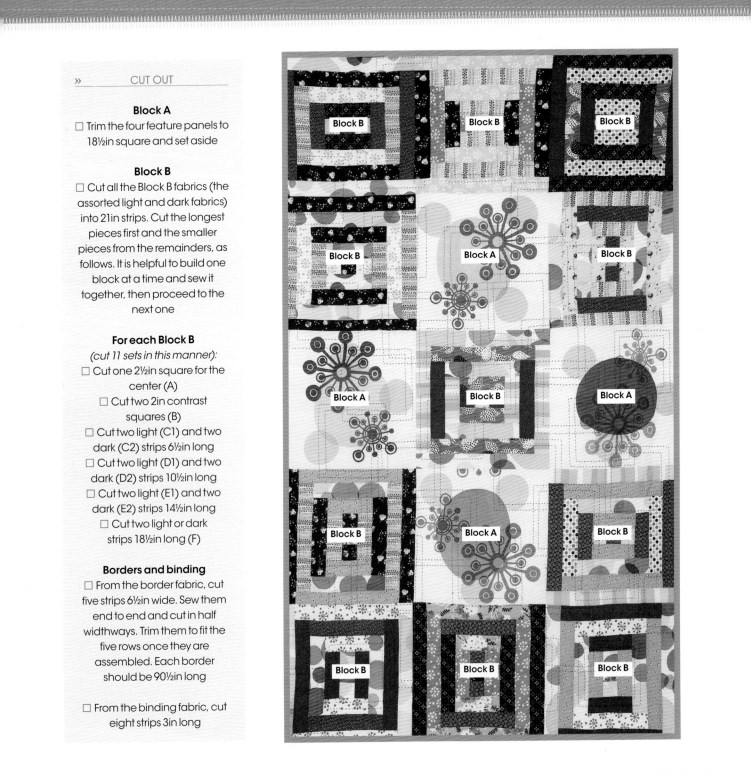

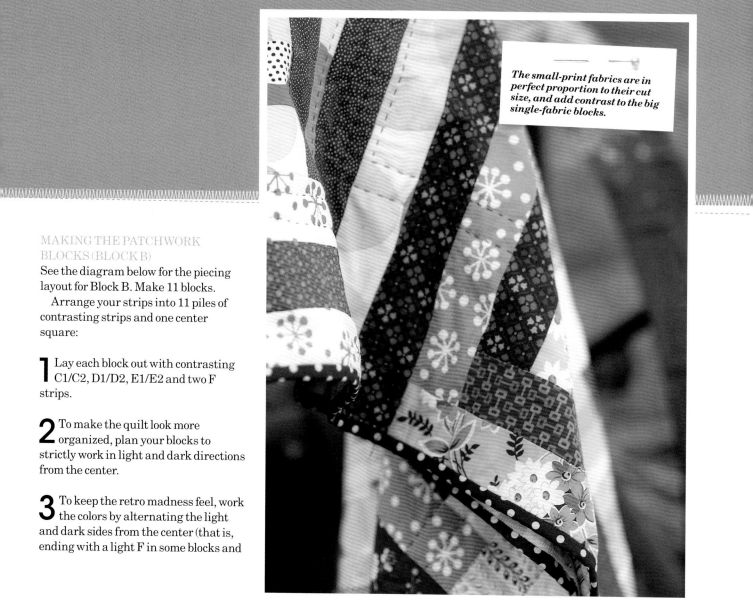

MAKING THE PATCHWORK BLOCKS (BLOCK B)

See the diagram below for the piecing layout for Block B. Make 11 blocks.

Arrange your strips into 11 piles of contrasting strips and one center square:

1 Lay each block out with contrasting C1/C2, D1/D2, E1/E2 and two F strips.

2 To make the quilt look more organized, plan your blocks to strictly work in light and dark directions from the center.

3 To keep the retro madness feel, work the colors by alternating the light and dark sides from the center (that is, ending with a light F in some blocks and

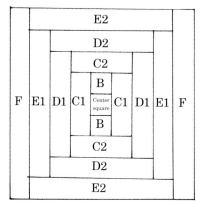

a dark F in others).

Start with a center square:
• Sew a B square to opposite sides of the center square
• Sew a C1 strip to both sides of this set
• Sew a C2 strip to both ends of this set
• Sew a D1 strip to both sides of this set
• Sew a D2 strip to both ends of this set
• Do the same with the E1 and E2 strips then finish with an F Strip on each side
• The finished block should be square and measure 18½in all around

Pages 78–83:
This project and all associated text, images and patterns are taken from *Material Obsession* by Kathy Doughty and Sarah Fielke, published by Murdoch Books. Visit www.murdochbooks.co.uk

QUILT CONSTRUCTION

Construct the body of the quilt by sewing five rows of three blocks.

Set out the feature panels in the center of rows 2 and 4 and on the ends of row 3 (refer to the photo of the full quilt on page 83).

BORDERS

1 Measure the length through the center of the quilt body.

2 Trim the border pieces to 90½in after checking to make sure your sewing is accurate.

3 Find the middle of the border strips and finger-press a crease. Now find the middle of the body of the quilt and finger-press a crease. Match these points and pin.

4 Pin the ends, then pin every few inches along the sides to allow for any variations.

5 Gently ease the edges as necessary to make them fit together. When you have made the borders fit perfectly, sew them on.

This method will ensure you achieve a flat border free of waves. Press flat, toward the borders. Press the entire quilt top carefully.

BACKING, QUILTING AND BINDING

When the top is complete, measure your backing fabric and cut to fit, allowing a little extra, and piecing it if necessary to get the right size.

See pages 23–26 for instructions on finishing.

TOP TIP
This quilt was hand-quilted by setting out the rectangles using masking tape and quilting around the inside and the outside of the tape with brown perle cotton. However, you could also quilt it yourself, or send it to a long arm quilter.

Whether hand or machine quilted, consider the style as it will be more visible over the single-fabric blocks.

A PASSION FOR PATCHWORK

Author and blogger Jane Brocket has been crafting nearly all her life, but became drawn to patchwork and quilting in more recent years and now there's just no stopping her...

Jane Brocket first came to the crafting world's attention through her popular blog, Yarnstorm. Packed with inspiring photos from everyday life, stunning craft projects and mouth-watering cakes and bakes, Jane's passion for color and pattern shines through on every entry. The blog's success has spawned several beautiful books by Jane, including *The Gentle Art of Quilt-Making*. We talked to Jane about her love of craft and passion for patchwork...

The Gentle Art of Quilt-Making by Jane Brocket.

COLLINS & BROWN

You've been crafting, baking and blogging for several years, but when did your love of crafting first evolve?

I started crafting when I was very young – I can't remember a time when I haven't been making things. I loved sticking and gluing and generally playing with materials. My Nana taught me to do very simple stitching when I was about four or five, and a student lodger taught me how to use an old Singer sewing machine when I was 11 (I made lots of smock-tops for myself), but it took me ages to learn how to knit, despite many attempts between the ages of seven and 19.

Quilting and patchwork are skills you've learned more recently – what inspired you to give them a go?

I only really started to like the idea of patchwork and quilting about 10 or 12 years ago. Until then, I have to admit that although I really loved the traditional nineteenth century and early twentieth century (up to the 1940s) patchworks and quilts, I really couldn't get excited by contemporary patchwork. I'd also been badly put off by hand-sewn hexagon patches at school and again when I started a course at a local college about 15 years ago.

Then I went to an exhibition of Kaffe Fassett quilts at the American Museum in Bath and was amazed by what he was doing with simple shapes and wonderful fabrics. The shop there was selling some of his newly launched quilt fabrics and they were what really started me quilting properly. I'd just been waiting for the right fabrics, apparently!

I then went on a weekend course to learn basic patchwork skills – mainly how to cut and piece, and how to use a rotary cutter, self-healing mat and quilter's ruler. It gave me all I needed to know to get started.

In your first book, **The Gentle Art of Domesticity,** *you quote DH Lawrence, who said 'the actual doing of things is in itself a joy'. What, for you, is the most exciting part of creating a patchwork design – selecting your fabrics, sewing it all together, or the satisfaction of seeing your finished project?*

My quilts are made in quite distinct phases, and I enjoy them all. When I'm thinking about the next quilt, I spend a long time planning it in my head (it can take months or years for me to decide what to do with lovely pieces of fabric).

When I have an idea for a quilt or want to use a specific fabric in a quilt, I bring together all the possible fabrics that might go into it. This is a really lovely part of the process, playing with the combinations, washing and ironing them, enjoying the designs and colors.

Once I've decided what I'm doing I cut out very swiftly – I don't dither – and then comes one of the best bits: laying out the pieces into a pleasing arrangement. I do this quickly, too, but leave the layout out on the floor for at least a day before machine-piecing so I can make alterations if necessary. For the next part, I am very happy sitting at my machine, sewing the top together while listening to Radio 4.

These days I really like making the back of a quilt. I used to just use one fabric, but now the backs of my quilts are getting more adventurous and like abstract quilt tops. Once the sandwich has been pinned (least favorite part), I enjoy hand-quilting the whole thing while watching films (anything with Cary Grant does nicely). I even like hand stitching the binding, as I know that by that stage it's nearly all done. Then there is the pleasure of seeing and using the finished quilt – I still get a nice surprise when I see some of the quilts I've made and remember favorite fabrics or moments of making.

How long does it take you to finish a patchwork quilt?

Once I've started a quilt, I work on it quite quickly, so I can make a machine-pieced, hand-quilted quilt in less than a week without feeling under pressure. Some simple quilts can be cut out in an afternoon, pieced the next day, made into a sandwich, and hand-quilted in a couple of evenings.

Jane is mainly inspired by gorgeous fabrics in the first instance, then she enjoys working out how to include them in a patchwork design.

"I went to an exhibition of Kaffe Fassett quilts and was amazed by what he was doing with simple shapes and wonderful fabrics"

Your blog is filled with beautiful photographs taken from everyday surroundings. You have a real talent for picking out interesting patterns and color from the sights of day-to-day life – have you always been this way, or has your love of craft given you a way to look at the world afresh?

I think I must have been looking at patterns and colors and textures all my life, but I didn't really become aware of it until I had children (Tom and Alice are now 19, Phoebe is 16). It was only then that I started seeing the world afresh and with new eyes, looking at things with them. I remember being ››

Jane will often base her designs on colors and patterns taken from the world around her. These rows of colorful sweet jars (below) inspired the fabric choices in her Candy quilt (left).

"For me, the trick is to use really lovely, exciting fabrics that do all the hard work of creating interest, and put them into very basic patterns"

fascinated by the children's books I was reading to them and the way the books and the children both observed and pointed out so many ordinary, everyday, but interesting details (for example, the Ahlbergs, Shirley Hughes, Sarah Garland and Quentin Blake).

You talk in your book about simplifying the quilting process – is it true that patchwork projects can be as complicated or easy as you decide to make them?

Yes, quilting can be just as hard or as easy as you like. Anyone who can cut out some squares or rectangles or strips of fabric, sew a straight line on a machine, and do some running stitch for quilting can make a simple quilt. If you use simple shapes (squares, rectangles,

strips) you can make a huge variety of quilts – in fact, I often say that even if you only ever used squares, you'd never run out of ideas and designs. For me, the trick is to use really lovely, exciting fabrics that do all the hard work of creating interest, and to put them into very basic patterns that show them off.

You often refer to Kaffe Fassett as an inspiration for your patchwork creations – what is it about his designs that you love?

The fact that when his books first appeared, the quilts in them were a breath of fresh air, full of color and energy and exuberance, and they introduced me to the idea that quilts could be wild and colorful, as well as simple and doable. He has a very can-do

approach, which inspired me to have a go after years of dithering and worrying about the end results. I realized, after seeing what he did, that I was being held back by a self-imposed idea that there was a 'right' way to do everything in quilting. I now know for sure that there is no correct way – just what works for you.

Are there any other contemporary quilt or patchwork designers you admire?

I tend to start with a fabric rather than a particular design, so I'm more inspired by fabric designers such as Lotta Jansdotter, Heather Ross, Denyse Schmidt, Martha Negley and Naomi Ito. I also love Philip Jacobs' fabric designs.

Where do you find all the fabrics you use for your patchwork projects? Do you recycle old fabric scraps or are you tempted by new designs?

See above, but I also recycle fabrics. I cut up old tablecloths, clothes, shirts, curtains and household linens. I buy as and when I see something I really like, or when I need something specific. The US undoubtedly has the best choice of quilting fabrics, and I buy online from eQuilter and Glorious Color. I also shop around and at the moment use the Eternal Maker in Chichester, which has an incredible range of fabrics with masses of Japanese designs. I also buy from the Cotton Patch in Birmingham, and from Ray Stitch in London. I buy some fabric on eBay, and love looking around the fabric shops in London.

Your new book, The Gentle Art of Stitching, comes out in September. Tell us more!

It's an exploration of simple, enjoyable, easygoing stitching in various different forms. Instead of focusing on one branch of stitching, it covers many (such as sashiko, kantha, quilting, vintage-style embroidery, classic stitches and cross stitch) and offers lots of ideas for different projects that can be done by anyone who can thread a needle and stitch a basic stitch. Nothing in the book takes forever, and all the projects are easy to finish.

What's next? Are you planning any more patchwork projects?

I'm in the middle of writing my second quilting book, which will be published in 2013, so I'm very much in the thick of it, surrounded by quilts and fabrics. I have to say, I really like writing quilting books!

Kristin Perers / Collins & Brown; Candy and all beach photos: Jane Brocket

BEACH HUT QUILTS

Jane talks us through the creation of the Candy and Ice-Cream versions of her seaside-inspired design

Inspiration

What I particularly like about beach huts is their home-made look, the fact that the best ones are personalized, painted in jaunty colors and clearly loved by their owners.

I also admire the way that their lines, being hand-painted and then weather-beaten, are not always perfect, and I enjoy the way they present a relaxed, uncoordinated character.

As for color, both quilts take inspiration from the seaside. The candy version contains colors we find in all the major British seaside resorts in summer, and the Ice-Cream version is deliberately paler and inspired by ice-creams sold in old-fashioned ice-cream parlours.

Design

I have been making detours to look at beach huts for years and have long wanted to make a simple quilted version, but was put off by the idea of needing a roof on each hut (and thus getting into the business of triangles). But after a walk on Whitstable beach, when I photographed the various stripes of the beach huts, I realized that it was these stripes that I wanted to use most of all. So I simplified and simplified the source of inspiration until I came to the four-stripe square blocks that are placed in an alternating horizontal and vertical pattern in the way that the directions of the beach hut stripes vary from hut to hut.

Fabrics

Ice-Cream quilt (right): This quilt took 'peaches and cream' as a first guiding principle and then branched out into ice-cream/sandy beach/dots of blue sky/pale sea colors until I had a very 'English beach in summer' or 'ice-cream parlour' effect. The majority of the fabrics lack real intensity of color – they are all very pretty versions of colors – but they are of the same tonal value.

Candy quilt (below): I discovered this was a great design for playing with color. It could be made in just two colors, the way many beach huts are painted, or you could restrict each square to two colors, but I decided to use some pink, blue and aqua fabrics. These make for a bright, sun-washed quilt with a few splashes of deeper yellows and deep marine blues.

see page 72
to make Jane's
Ice-Cream quilt…

The bold stripes of beach huts proved a great pattern for Jane to base her design on, with endless options for vibrant fabric and color choices.

This page: all text and images are taken from *The Gentle Art of Quilt-Making* by Jane Brocket, published by Collins & Brown

GALLERY

Tesco Direct

GIRL'S WALL MURAL
Wallpaper King

B ring warmth, color and texture into your living spaces in an instant with pretty patchwork makes. From quirky cushions, to large quilts and throws – whatever your skill level, there'll be a project to give your home a personal touch. In this section you'll find plenty of ideas you can try, so be inspired to get creative!

COLORFUL FLORAL PATCHWORK
Kingsize Quilt by Coast and Country Interiors, Not On The High Street

BRIGHT IDEAS
get the look everywhere

Sew together some pretty, **vintage-style tea towels** to make a quirky dining room table cloth.

Give **kitchen tiles** the patchwork treatment! Either mix and match when adding new tiles, or use special tile paint to add the effect to existing ones.

Bathroom curtains don't have to be boring. A simple **patchwork café curtain** brings rustic chic (and modesty!) to a luxurious soak in the tub.

Add a patched trim to existing **plain bedding** to brighten it up - a smart way to use up small fabric scraps.

Experiment with **wallpaper samples** – the kids' bedroom is a great place to try this – just mix & match over a small area for a fun random effect!

flight of fancy

Perfect for Easter or all-year-round, we think these pretty hanging birds would add a charming decorative touch to a nursery or children's bedroom. Each bird is worked in a patchwork design featuring ribbon and button detail.
Set Of Six Patchwork Bird Decorations, Dot Com Gift Shop

ideal for YOUR HOME

Give your living spaces the full patchwork treatment!

Pick a color!

COOL BRITANNIA

The trend for all-things British shows no signs of abating, and these Union Flag cushions will add a 'perfectly patriotic' feel to your living room.
Red and Green Patchwork Union Jack Cushions, Dot Com Gift Shop

MINI ADVENTURE

Patchwork needn't just be made from fabric – this cool Mini print would add a retro vibe to a room and its bright and bold shades will give instant lift to your home décor scheme. The design is based on an original mixed media artwork printed on quality cardstock.
Patchwork Mini Print, Tula Moon

country charm

Who knew a doorstop could be so attractive? A posy of felt flowers fill this patchwork pot to create a must-have accessory for the home that's both pretty and practical.
Floral Bunch Doorstop, Laura Ashley

OH SO PRETTY!

We think this lovely floral patchwork mug will be just your cup to tea! Its delicate mix of floral fabric patterns and trimmings are guaranteed to brighten up your morning.

Stripey Paisley Park Mug, Dot Com Gift Shop

Kitchen classic!

cool beans

Having friends over for coffee? Serve the most stylish hot drinks they've ever seen using this vibrant cafetiere cozy, complete with flouncy rosette! A must-buy for any caffeine addict!

Patchwork Cafetiere Cozy, www.ulsterweavers.com

COZY CUPPA

As if you'd ever need an extra excuse for a tea break, this wonderful patchwork bus tea cozy comes in two sizes, small and regular – so no matter how much you love a good brew, you'll have things covered!

Bus Tea Cozy, Poppy Treffry

Bright idea!

WALL TO WALL

We just can't believe this amazing digital wallpaper, exclusive to Cath Kidston, who photograph their favorite vintage fabrics and artwork, then print the digital images on to high-quality paper. If you're potty about patchwork, then this very special wallpaper is worth saving up for.

Patchwork Digital Wallpaper, Cath Kidston

apple a day

A cute gift idea that looks good enough to eat! These adorable patchwork hanging apples are topped off with ribbon loops and felt leaves. ***Set Of Six Quilted Patchwork Apple Decorations, Dot Com Gift Shop***

ideas FOR GIFTS

Share your passion for patchwork with your loved ones, with our selection of cool gift ideas – each with a quilting or patchwork twist!

Cute idea!

WHAT A DOLL

The perfect gift for a craft-mad pal, this oh-so-cute Russian Doll pendant is handmade and comes with a 24" silver plated chain. Why not buy two – one for a friend and one for yourself? ***Russian Doll Pendant, Tula Moon***

take note

Be inspired by traditional hexagonal patchwork design – this charming notebook is covered in a classic quilted print, and makes a fun present for a pal who loves fabric patterns, or who needs a patchwork project planner book. ***Patchwork Notebook, Petra Boase***

EASY E-READ

Book lovers can pack up their portable library with ease, thanks to this charming Kindle cover in a luxury patchwork design. Each case is different, and handmade by designer Nicky Louth Davies. ***Patchwork Kindle Case, wowthankyou.co.uk/nicky-louth-davies***

**PETIT PAN
PATCHWORK
CUSHIONS**

Petit Home

Lay your stash out and **mix & match** fabrics at random - you'll be amazed at how great the most unlikely combinations look!

No scrap of fabric is too small - from **bright bunting** to covered buttons, you never know when those off-cuts will come into their own.

Most of us have at least one pair of jeans that we don't wear - pick them apart and make them into a **hard wearing bag** for life instead (see page 60).

Fancy getting crafty in front of the TV? Try a bit of **hand sewing** - perfect for achieving the shabby chic look (and keeping an eye on the kids!)

Anything goes with patchwork, so let your imagination go wild and choose a kaleidoscope of strong fabric patterns to give your makes a contemporary look. Patchwork is perfect for making fun accessories, such as these sweet storage pockets, or even works beautifully as a base for quirky toys! And as you get to choose your fabric squares, it's so easy to select colors and patterns that will look stunning in the setting you have in mind.

**PATCHWORK
CUSHION**

*Jane Foster
Design*

Original Stitch

Heart to heart

Featuring a triple heart design this pretty little keyring is a cute smaller gift for a special friend.

At such a small price tag, you can afford to buy several to keep ready for up-coming birthdays.

Triple Heart Patchwork Keyring, Sass and Belle

MAGNETIC CHARM

Stuck for a fun gift for a crafting friend? Try these cute fridge magnets – they're a sweet way of adding a touch of country charm to a kitchen.
Home Sweet Home Magnetic Letters, Live Laugh Love

Pretty & practical

time for tea

We just love the quirky style of Poppy Treffry's appliqué designs. Her work now features on a range of gifts and homewares, including a collection of mouth-watering die-cut greetings cards.
Tea & Biscuits Die-Cut Greetings Card, Poppy Treffry

Send with love

HAPPY CAMPER

How cute is this card? Sporting a retro-patchwork design, the VW camper van on this card has become a design classic.
The card is blank for you to add your own message.
Patchwork Camper Van Greetings Card, Tula Moon

CRAFTY CALLS

We want these! iPhone cases and covers featuring fabulous patchwork designs make great gifts for crafting friends, or you might want to keep one all to yourself!
Front: Fabric Patchwork iPhone 4 Speckcase, Zazzle,
Back: Vintage Wave Patchwork iPhone 4 Case, Quilt My Phone

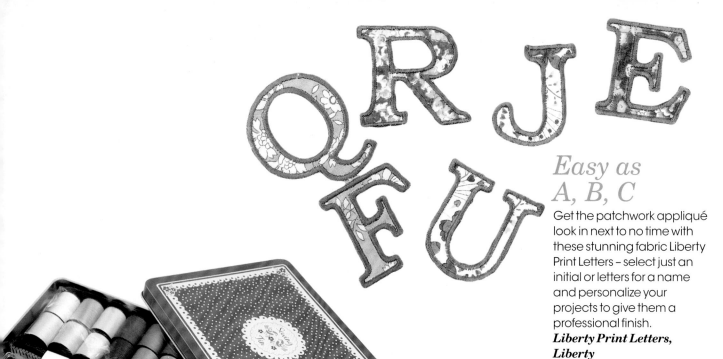

Easy as A, B, C

Get the patchwork appliqué look in next to no time with these stunning fabric Liberty Print Letters – select just an initial or letters for a name and personalize your projects to give them a professional finish.
Liberty Print Letters, Liberty

Sew PERFECT

Indulge in these sewing accessories and fabrics to add that little extra something to your patchwork projects

Cute & useful!

VINTAGE VIBE

Filled with everything a sewing newbie could possibly need, this deluxe sewing kit, based in a cute retro-style tin, contains 15 cotton reels, a thread picker, mini pin cushion, needle book and much more!

Vintage Doily Deluxe Sewing Kit, Dot Com Gift Shop

HOME SWEET HOME

Store your plans and fabric swatches for your future patchwork projects in this handy journal. It features eight fill-in sections and durable pockets to store swatches and clippings. Each section contains space to dream up the perfect room, create project and shopping lists, floor plans, and keep track of measurements.
Home Ideas Journal, Cath Kidston

Jot it down!

ALL THE TRIMMINGS

Mmmm! The yummy array of trimmings in this gift tin will have any keen crafter eager to delve inside! Or if you are needing to spare the pennies, you can always buy your trimmings separately.

The Trimmings Tin, Seam Star; Extra Large Ric-Rac, Millie Moon; Sky Blue Pom-Pom Bobble Trim, Sew Là Là

Ready to sew!

BUNDLES OF JOY

Get a load of gorgeous prints all in one go, with a patchwork bundle packed with patterns pre-selected to work well together. The Liberty bundle contains enough strips to make a 130 x 185cm quilt and the Cath Kidston bundle has eight pieces of classic print fabric.

Patchwork Bundle, Liberty; Haberdashery Cotton Patchwork Squares, Cath Kidston

bags of style

Craft bags needn't be boring, as this striking Cath Kidston design goes to show. Featuring her Royal Rose print, the spacious bag contains two compartments, to keep your projects in order and several pockets for stashing away smaller bits and bobs.
Royal Rose Craft Bag, Cath Kidston

More Great Books from Design Originals

All My Thanks & Love to Quilts
ISBN: 978-1-57421-425-3 **$24.99**
DO5396

Five-Minute Quilt Blocks
ISBN: 978-1-57421-420-8 **$18.99**
DO5391

Crazy Quilt Christmas Stockings
ISBN: 978-1-57421-360-7 **$8.99**
DO3483

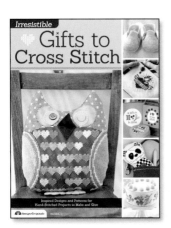

Irresistible Gifts to Cross Stitch
ISBN: 978-1-57421-445-1 **$19.99**
DO5416

10 Minute Quilt Blocks
ISBN: 978-1-57421-669-1 **$16.99**
DO5358

Sew Baby
ISBN: 978-1-57421-421-5 **$19.99**
DO5392

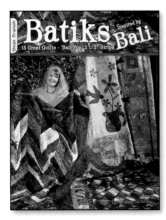

Batiks Inspired By Bali
ISBN: 978-1-57421-652-3 **$24.99**
DO5341

Zen-sational Stitches for Quilting
ISBN: 978-1-57421-406-2 **$18.99**
DO5377

Steampunk Your Wardrobe
ISBN: 978-1-57421-417-8 **$19.99**
DO5388